Pr

"Need-to-read inside inforr the best source in the busin

"The Inside the Minds serie techniques of accomplished professionals..." – Chuck Birenbaum, Partner, Thelen Reid & Priest

"Aspatore has tapped into a gold mine of knowledge and expertise ignored by other publishing houses." – Jack Barsky, Managing Director, Information Technology & Chief Information Officer, ConEdison *Solutions*

"Unlike any other publisher – actual authors that are on the front-lines of what is happening in industry." – Paul A. Sellers, Executive Director, National Sales, Fleet and Remarketing, Hyundai Motor America

"A snapshot of everything you need..." – Charles Koob, Co-Head of Litigation Department, Simpson Thacher & Bartlet

"Everything good books should be - honest, informative, inspiring, and incredibly well-written." – Patti D. Hill, President, BlabberMouth PR

"Great information for both novices and experts." – Patrick Ennis, Partner, ARCH Venture Partners

"A rare peek behind the curtains and into the minds of the industry's best." – Brandon Baum, Partner, Cooley Godward

"Intensely personal, practical advice from seasoned dealmakers." – Mary Ann Jorgenson, Coordinator of Business Practice Area, Squire, Sanders & Dempsey

"Great practical advice and thoughtful insights." – Mark Gruhin, Partner, Schmeltzer, Aptaker & Shepard, PC

"Reading about real-world strategies from real working people beats the typical business book hands down." - Andrew Ceccon, Chief Marketing Officer, OnlineBenefits Inc.

"Books of this publisher are syntheses of actual experiences of real-life, hands-on, front-line leaders--no academic or theoretical nonsense here. Comprehensive, tightly organized, yet nonetheless motivational!" - Lac V. Tran, Sr. Vice President, CIO and Associate Dean Rush University Medical Center

"Aspatore is unlike other publishers...books feature cutting-edge information provided by top executives working on the front-line of an industry." - Debra Reisenthel, President and CEO, Novasys Medical Inc

ASPATORE

www.Aspatore.com

Aspatore Books, a Thomson Reuters business, exclusively publishes C-Level executives (CEO, CFO, CTO, CMO, Partner) from the world's most respected companies and law firms. C-Level Business Intelligence™, as conceptualized and developed by Aspatore Books, provides professionals of all levels with proven business intelligence from industry insiders—direct and unfiltered insight from those who know it best—as opposed to third-party accounts offered by unknown authors and analysts. Aspatore Books is committed to publishing an innovative line of business and legal books, those which lay forth principles and offer insights that when employed, can have a direct financial impact on the reader's business objectives, whatever they may be. In essence, Aspatore publishes critical tools for all business professionals.

Inside the Minds

The *Inside the Minds* series provides readers of all levels with proven legal and business intelligence from C-Level executives and lawyers (CEO, CFO, CTO, CMO, Partner) from the world's most respected companies and law firms. Each chapter is comparable to a white paper or essay and is a future-oriented look at where an industry, profession, or topic is heading and the most important issues for future success. Each author has been selected based upon their experience and C-Level standing within the professional community. *Inside the Minds* was conceived in order to give readers actual insights into the leading minds of top lawyers and business executives worldwide, presenting an unprecedented look at various industries and professions.

INSIDE THE MINDS

Working with Government Agencies in Government Contracts Law

Leading Lawyers on Managing Compliance Issues, Securing a Contract, and Communicating with Key Agencies

ASPATORE

Mat #40838783

Inside the Minds Project Manager, Caitlin Keiper; edited by Eddie Fournier; proofread by Melanie Zimmerman

---

ISBN 978-0-314-19941-6

For corrections, updates, comments or any other inquiries please e-mail TLR.AspatoreEditorial@thomson.com.

First Printing, 2009
10 9 8 7 6 5 4 3 2 1

Contents

Eric W. Leonard **7**
Partner, **Wiley Rein LLP**
THE KEY COMPONENTS OF GOVERNMENT CONTRACTS LAW

William C. Bergmann **35**
Partner, **Baker Hostetler LLP**
GOVERNMENT CONTRACTS LAW AND INTELLECTUAL PROPERTY RIGHTS

Steven D. Weinstein **57**
Partner, **Blank Rome LLP**
CONTRACTS AND BIDDING ON THE STATE AND LOCAL GOVERNMENT LEVEL: KEY CONSIDERATIONS

Matthew Koehl **73**
Partner, **K&L Gates LLP**
NEW STRATEGIES AND CHALLENGES FOR GOVERNMENT CONTRACTORS

Appendices **91**

The Key Components of Government Contracts Law

Eric W. Leonard

Partner

Wiley Rein LLP

ASPATORE

The Key Agencies

A wide variety of agencies or related entities monitor and enforce government contract law in the pre-award, performance, and post-award stages of the contracting cycle. In my practice on the enforcement side, we tend to deal primarily with the agency inspector general's offices within a given agency, the Defense Criminal Investigative Service, and the Department of Justice. Other entities can affect enforcement decisions and conduct their own investigations relating to government contracts, such as the Department of Labor investigators, the Office of Federal Contract Compliance Programs, and others. Each of these entities possesses substantial subpoena powers to investigate civil and/or criminal allegations of violations of federal law. In addition, the Defense Contract Audit Agency provides audits and oversight support to Department of Defense agencies, as well as some civilian agencies (when the Defense Contract Audit Agency is requested to provide such assistance).

Furthermore, the Court of Federal Claims and Government Accountability Office are responsible for enforcing federal procurement competition requirements imposed by the Competition in Contracting Act. Typically, this enforcement proceeding will take the form of bid protest litigation. Similarly, agency boards of contract appeals have jurisdiction to hear disputes (such as contract claims) under the Contract Disputes Act, and can play a role in ensuring compliance with government contract administration rules.

Many times, the agency that provides the oversight and enforcement of a certain contract is driven by which agency awards the contract under which the enforcement issue arose. Sometimes, however, certain types of issues or disputes that arise under a contract are handled by specific entities. For instance, the Department of Justice (both through lawyers at the department and assistant U.S. attorneys) typically handles *qui tam* (also known as whistleblower) actions and criminal grand jury matters. Similarly, it is not unusual for an agency contracting officer or other official to refer matters to the outside enforcement entities such as the U.S. Attorney's Office if there is an allegation involving possible criminal conduct.

Each agency has its own procurement rules typically codified in supplements to the Federal Acquisition Regulation (FAR)—the "bible" of government contract law—and internal guidance/memos. Each agency also has its own particular mission and acquisition needs (e.g., services versus product, security considerations, etc.) that will drive its procurement decisions. In fact, each federal agency effectively acts as a separate business or corporation, and the level of expertise of an agency's procurement personnel varies. While it is not always fair to paint with a broad brush, my experience has shown that Department of Defense agencies tend to have more seasoned contracting professionals, while at times civilian agencies can lag behind in terms of expertise and familiarity with the FAR. Unfortunately, understaffing (resulting in overworked and overloaded contract professionals) and an aging workforce present significant challenges for many federal contracting activities (both on the Department of Defense and civilian agency sides). These pressures (confirmed by many recent studies and reports prepared externally and within the government) have brought about vigorous recruitment efforts by many federal agencies.

In today's procurement environment, with the United States fighting two wars abroad, many factors can affect the urgency of working with these agencies—especially defense agencies. Listed below are some typical factors beyond mere contract performance and agency requirements that have affected recent particular procurement deals, processes, disputes, and enforcement matters we have handled:

- Unique mission-sensitive urgent needs of an agency
- Security concerns/needs
- Political/Capitol Hill influences and issues
- Understaffing at agencies
- Appropriated funds pressures

Developing Relationships with Agencies

In the world of government contracts, federal contractors (generally with the assistance of legal counsel) tend to litigate against the government typically through the bid protest litigation or claims process. Nevertheless, we always strive to craft an acceptable business solution to a contract dispute first, especially one that would allow agency counterparts to "save face" whenever possible. This is particularly true in protests. Indeed, we have seen a greater willingness of agency personnel to consider and sometimes accede to settlements that involve varying degrees of corrective action, such as reopening the bidding process or splitting the contract between the awardees and the protester. This result avoids the uncertainty of the litigation and costs associated with the pursuing litigation. We also find that some contract disputes get bogged down at the contracting officer level. Parallel discussions with agency counsel can be an effective counterpart to interactions between our clients and their government customers at the contracting or program level.

As is true in most any business environment/interaction, it is critical to earn the respect and trust of your adversary or customer. We have seen first-hand the impact a deteriorating relationship can have on the ability of a contractor and the government to resolve a lingering contract dispute. For instance, in a recent case, the relationship between my client and its customer had broken down over performance issues, and that led to an ongoing dispute over whether there had been performance deficiencies on one side, and whether the government owed the contractor additional consideration on the other. As each side became more entrenched in its position, they both lost the ability to reach an amicable solution. Only after the issue came to the edge of litigation did our client turn to us. Fortunately, we were able to navigate around the personalities that had been subjectively involved in the dispute at the ground level and reach out to the government's attorneys. We ultimately cooperated with senior procurement officials and were able to cultivate a fresh, new relationship that was not soured by the bitter dispute that had taken place. Once we were able to negotiate with a fresh relationship, both parties quickly settled the dispute.

Relationships also can be critical to achieving a successful solution in the context of government investigations. For instance, we recently handled a broad investigation resulting from the filing of a *qui tam* complaint. Based on an existing relationship of trust between adversaries and a well-developed working relationship (cultivated over the years), the government investigator in the case reached out to us on an informal basis and shared the elements of the complaint in order to give us (and the client) a chance early on in the government's investigation to convince the government why the allegations lacked merit. In this matter, we even were able to avoid issuance of a subpoena—a tool typically used by investigators to gather information in the early stages of an investigation. As a result, rather than force our client to incur the large expense of preparing a subpoena response, we were given the opportunity to meet with the investigators and convince them why the case had no merit—something we were able to do after only a few meetings. In fact, we were able to successfully close down the case in under a year with no payment from the client—an unusual result for these types of matters.

The contractor is responsible for managing its day-to-day relationship with its customer, and the quality of that relationship is often dictated by the contractor's performance and ability to deliver as promised. Timely, on-budget, successful performance often breeds good relationships with the government. On the other hand, when there is a breakdown in the quality, schedule, or cost, the government is usually receptive to justified business solutions if the contractor is willing to take responsibility for problems it has caused or contributed to. Inevitably, sometimes this results in the contractor assuming responsibility for problems that were created or contributed to by the government, in order to preserve the relationship and maintain the business partnership.

On the whole, the government procurement workforce is stressed to its limit, and that presents its own challenges to developing an effective working relationship. Recent studies and reports have found that the government is severely understaffed in agency procurement circles and that hiring is necessary, especially at the contracting officer technical representative and contracting office levels. It remains to be seen, however, how successful hiring efforts will be and whether other solutions (like increased outsourcing of certain government functions) may need to be considered to alleviate this issue. At the same time, resource consumption through recent increased regulation and scrutiny of the government contracting industry threatens to exacerbate this problem. These factors combine to create an ever-increasing strain on the government's procurement resources. The net result is that it is not unusual for contractors and their lawyers to not receive prompt decisions necessary to resolve a dispute, claim, or ongoing investigation matter. This is frustrating for clients and is an area that hopefully would improve if more resources are hired (or functions outsourced) by agencies.

Inter-Agency Cooperation

Inter-agency cooperation can be a useful tool to streamline the procurement process, and one way to secure this support is through the use of inter-agency agreements to facilitate purchasing, typically through large acquisition vehicles like CIO-SP2 and GSA Schedules. While use of these vehicles was robust for years, recent procurement "scandals" (such as the high-profile procurement of interrogator services under a GSA Schedule and other contracting arrangements that, arguably, have "pushed the envelope" in terms of scope of services available under a GSA Schedule contract) and resulting criticisms have hampered efforts to promote and expand the use of such purchasing vehicles. Instead, agencies have been developing their own acquisition vehicles through which the agency can issue task orders to awardees.

As noted earlier, however, we have seen increased willingness in agencies to work together cooperatively toward finding a mutually acceptable resolution in the investigation, contract disputes, and claims and protest areas. We also have seen a large increase in the use of alternative dispute resolution procedures to resolve contractual disputes between government contractors and agencies, particularly at the agency Board of Contract Appeals. Cooperative efforts with the Department of Justice to settle or resolve allegations of fraud, raised by a *qui tam* plaintiff or otherwise, are also more prevalent. However, the fact that the workforce in federal government is stretched to its limits can hinder the ability of agency personnel to set aside time to work cooperatively when issues arise.

We do see increasing state and federal collaboration as well. Many state and local governments have their own procurement laws and regulations that are applicable to state and local procurements. These statutes and regulations vary in terms of complexity and depth of procurement rules, but they are all loosely modeled on the federal procurement rules model, the FAR. Navigating these state and local procurement rules can be a challenge (especially in the context of a bid protest at the state/local level), but cooperation between state/local and federal purchasing processes is on the rise. This is exemplified by state and local purchasing of GSA Schedule 70 contracts for certain information technology requirements and similar purchasing for certain disaster recovery needs. Still, it is important to stress that the state and federal procurement purchasing systems are otherwise separate procurement systems.

Developing a Client's Primary Goal

The primary goals of any federal contractor are to increase revenue and profitability and expand market share, while at the same time building a reputation for superior performance. Our goal as counselors to these companies is to employ whatever lawful means are appropriate to achieve both these goals (which at times certainly can be in conflict). To achieve these goals, it is critical at the inception of the procurement process for companies to carefully consider the proposed terms and conditions of the procurement opportunity. In other words, companies need to identify the contract "baseline" both in terms of scope/nature of the product or services sought and under what terms and conditions the government seeks this product or service. These factors will drive the requirements (both legal and performance-related) that will be incorporated into the contract as awarded as well as the level of compliance and performance risk associated with the opportunity. This can be a very tricky inquiry, especially if the decision to bid or not is blindly tied to the revenue or profit angle or the procurement is designated by management as a company "must win" for one reason or another. The worst possible situation for a federal contractor is to over-promise what it can deliver or agree to contract terms and conditions it knows or should know it cannot satisfy.

If the contract is awarded to a company under such conditions, this course can result in default termination of the awarded contract by the government. This action could severely affect a company's ability to compete in future acquisitions and, more importantly, to "win" new business. As a result, it is essential for companies to develop accurate, unambiguous proposals in response to agency solicitations. They must also carefully monitor performance to maximize the likelihood of delivering what the company promised in its proposal. Finally, undertaking efforts to open the channels of communication early and often with agency counterparts to better understand agency expectations (of course, only when permitted under applicable law) is another way to help achieve the above objectives.

Early and open communication during contract performance is critical. Contractors need to have a process in place for detecting, raising, and addressing issues that arise in connection with a specific procurement so a company can be proactive when addressing such a situation. For instance, we have seen companies utilize comprehensive risk management databases that, in the general sense, can be effective tools to detect risks. However, we were also involved in one situation where a contractor developed an expensive, robust risk detection system to use on a high dollar value and highly visible procurement. While the system did a reasonably good job of capturing performance risks in real time, the system inexplicably lacked a process for communicating identified risks to company management so they could be assessed and addressed at higher levels within the company. In fact, neither upper management nor legal counsel was permitted to have access to the database. So while this contractor employed a great tool for identifying risk, the tool did little to help stave off performance disputes or permit management to make informed decisions about how and when to address identified risks. The result was protracted and expensive litigation to resolve what may have been otherwise preventable contract disputes.

Preparing the Client

A client's level of experience with its government agency customer and degree of interaction with that customer can vary substantially. We have found that sometimes companies that have worked with an agency for fifteen years have very little insight into the agency's procurement practices. On the whole, contractors that regularly deal with the Department of Defense tend to be the most sophisticated government contractors. In part, this may be attributable to the fact that Department of Defense contractors rely on the government for a larger percentage of their business (if not exclusive), and deal with a single procurement sector. Other contractors that may provide goods and/or services that are marketed to both commercial and government clients and, within the government, to both defense and civilian agencies are likely less government contract-centric than certain Department of Defense contractors.

We advise clients looking to enter into the federal marketplace or expand their presence within the federal marketplace, to consider carefully both business and legal/compliance issues. While the list of issues can be large depending on the complexity of the work the company has decided to undertake, below are a few broad areas of consideration:

Business Considerations

- Identify the nature of the competitive marketplace for the product or service you want to offer to the government.
- Identify the scope and nature of proposed work.
    - Product or service?
    - Large business or small business?
    - Be a prime contractor or subcontractor?
    - Limit to commercial item or do work subject to the cost accounting standards?
- Identify your company's risk tolerance.

Legal/Compliance Considerations

- Develop a comprehensive compliance checklist that details the scope of federal statutes and regulations that will be implicated by your business.
- Identify internal accounting and related system changes that will be necessary to support billings under federal contracts.
- Draft and implement a compliance plan/program (including a code of conduct) for new contractors that covers ethics, performance, socioeconomic/reporting, security, and discipline/violation reporting.
- Also analyze company-specific issues that could present compliance challenges, including company culture or decentralization. (Most federal contractors have a centralized structure.)

As noted earlier, different agency-specific rules will apply to each agency, usually in the form of a supplement to the FAR, and each agency will have different business needs. The business and legal checklists for a prospective federal contractor will vary for a variety of reasons, such as the scope of services/nature of product to be provided, the intended role of contractor (prime or subcontractor), and the amount of risk the company is willing to assume while operating in this environment. Companies also need to be cognizant that each contract incorporates a different mix of standard FAR contract clauses, so the client must be aware of unique requirements presented in any given contract. Companies also must be aware that these requirements can change during contract performance as applicable government contracts statutes or regulations can be amended or deleted.

Challenges in Securing a Contract

Some of the many factors that impact obtaining a government contract include price/cost, technical solution, past performance, and overall ability to demonstrate in a proposal that your company can provide the best solution to meet the agency's needs at a fair and reasonable price. After receiving a contract award, there are a multitude of potential barriers to effective completion of a contract, including stakeholder tensions, changes in the agency needs (we saw this happen on a number of contracts affected by the events of September 11, 2001), over-promising by a contractor in its proposal, and these are just a few. By way of example, we were recently brought in to assist a contractor get back on track with its performance in a multibillion-dollar procurement. In that case, the biggest challenge was "too many cooks in the kitchen." There were too many distinct performance sites with distinct (and disagreeing) stakeholders, and each had differing demands that adversely affected the client's ability to deliver a unified solution in a timely fashion. This, in turn, dramatically increased the cost of performance on this fixed-price contract, resulting in erosion of profit and the potential for placing the company in a loss contract situation. While in this case many of the problems were customer-created and -driven, the company had no choice but to work collaboratively with the customer, and together we were able to craft a workable and financially acceptable solution.

Similarly, the perception of "issues" under a contract (whether or not such issues exist) can be a challenge, and is one that can be quite difficult to resolve. For instance, we handled one matter where the agency customer was absolutely convinced our client was making a huge profit on the contract when in fact the company's profit was in line with what it had proposed, if not below that amount. This inaccurate perception caused significant issues and general distrust between the parties that culminated in the commencement of a costly investigation. While the investigation was eventually resolved favorably, our client still had the substantial legal and discovery-related costs of the investigation. This project, like others we handle, was complicated further by involvement from stakeholders on Capitol Hill. We have seen such involvement more and more on high-profile, large projects, and it can adversely affect contract performance as well as the ability to resolve any outstanding disputes. This involvement can be particularly troublesome to deal with if it involves political actors that are not familiar with federal procurement statutes and regulations.

Trends and Changes

A few recent noteworthy trends have affected (and will continue to affect) government contractors. First, over the past few years there has been a renewed focus on government contracts compliance and emphasis on the need for effective compliance/internal controls programs for government contractors. Recent FAR rules mandated that government contractors implement compliance programs and enhanced internal control mechanisms to detect fraud, violations of federal procurement laws, and material overpayments. See *Contractor Business Ethics Compliance Program and Disclosure Requirements*, FAR Case 2207-006, Final Rule, 73 Fed. Reg. 67064-02, 2008 WL 4861443 (Nov. 12, 2008), effective December 12, 2008. These rules will require mandatory disclosure to agency inspector generals anytime a contractor has "credible evidence" of a substantial overpayment, violation of certain criminal laws, or violation of the civil False Claims Act in connection with the performance, award, or close-out of a contract. Failure by a contractor to disclose covered conduct where there is credible evidence of a violation could subject the contractor to suspension or debarment for a minimum of three years. These rules also add/enhance certain internal controls requirements for certain federal contractors and subcontractors. As a result, we have seen increased emphasis and activity in this area, and we expect there will be greater enforcement activity.

Even before adoption of this new FAR rule, enforcement activity in connection with federal contracts and subcontracts had already increased over the past few years. In fact, since late 2006, a Department of Justice Procurement Fraud Task Force has been in place and staffed throughout the country. This task force has investigated many high-profile contracting issues, including ones involving the so-called "alliance contracting litigation"—an ongoing litigation that has affected hundreds of federal contractors. Similar large-scale investigations are ongoing relating to perceived waste, fraud, and abuse in connection with Iraq reconstruction and Katrina contracts. While it remains to be seen how these investigations unfold, there is little doubt that the era of enforcement has once again emerged in the government contracting industry, and that federal contractors need to be aware of this increased level of scrutiny.

Second, there has been significant scrutiny on commercial item contractors and, more specifically, the scope of the commercial item contracting rules. In recent years, the Air Force has moved away from commercial item contracting involved in major systems acquisitions (see Department of Defense Contracting: Efforts Needed to Address Air Force Commercial Acquisition Risk, GAO-06-995, 2006 WL 2803081, Sept. 2006), and is shifting its acquisition approach toward a non-commercial acquisition focus. Broader efforts also have emerged to restrict the "of a type" exception to commercial item definitions in the FAR so that only items that are actually sold, leased, or licensed to the general public could qualify as commercial items, but to date no changes to this language in the FAR have been implemented. The primary advantage of being a commercial item contractor is that companies that perform under commercial item contracts are exempt from many government contract statutes and regulations, such as the obligation to provide certified cost and pricing data or be subject to the cost accounting standards. As a result, these contractors take on less risk and many times can provide products and services to the government at prices competitive with what they would find in the commercial marketplace.

The third trend stems from the fact that the government now spends more on procuring services than purchasing products from federal contractors. This dramatic growth in service contracting has raised numerous challenges, including how to address agency use (or overuse) of time and materials contracts to fulfill its needs, expanded use of GSA Schedule vehicles for large services procurements, application and interpretation of the Service

Contract Act to more procurements, and use of broad "commercial services" definition to encompass services "of a type" offered in the commercial marketplace. These are just a few of the emerging issues associated with service contracting, but they serve to emphasize the fact that government rules and regulations need to adjust (and in some cases are adjusting) to the fact that the government now purchases more services than products on an annual basis from federal contractors.

To address many of these changes (particularly in the compliance areas), there is a need for contractors to dedicate resources and a critical need for attention from management to ensure full compliance in changed areas of the law. For changes like those described above relating to commercial item contracting (that as of yet have not involved any change in the law, but instead a change in agency business practices), companies may need to adjust their business strategies/practices to preserve market share and satisfy changing customer needs. For instance, given the tightening of commercial item practices, it now can be much harder for a company to flourish if it depends wholly on receiving commercial item contract awards. The reality is that we see more awards that previously were done on a FAR Part 12 commercial item basis now being made pursuant to FAR Part 15 as negotiated procurements.

Companies need to be constantly monitoring these changes or hire a government contract lawyer for that purpose, especially with the administration change that may bring about even more pronounced changes. Companies that fail to monitor changes in the statutory and regulatory government contracting environment do so at their own peril. Penalties for non-compliance in the government contract world are much more severe than in the commercial marketplace, and include substantial monetary penalties (see the False Claims Act), as well as the potential for suspension or debarment, which would prevent a government contractor from participating in the industry at all.

Below is a summarizing list of trends having the greatest impact on my practice over the past few years:

- Government contract compliance changes/mandatory disclosure and internal controls added requirements

- Tightening of the interpretation/application of the commercial item rules
- Changes in the rules governing specialty metals restrictions
- Expansion of protest jurisdiction to include protests of certain task orders awards
- Boom in services-related work purchased by the government, resulting in a greater need for expertise necessarily related to service contracting (including interpretation/application of the Service Contract Act and related statutes)
- Increased enforcement/investigation in the wake of perceived contracting abuses

Conflicts in Government Contracts Law

Investigations

Investigations and enforcement proceedings are handled in a variety of ways, since there is a wide variety of enforcement options and tools available to investigators. The type of enforcement proceeding initiated can take many forms and combinations, such as *qui tam* litigation, Defense Contract Audit Agency audit, contract action or termination, criminal charges, civil charges, inspector general or grand jury subpoena proceedings, federal trial, and/or suspension/debarment proceedings. How they are handled depends on the underlying facts, allegations, statutes implicated (i.e., is there mandatory disclosure, etc.), agency involved, and other factors. See Appendix A, a June 2008 presentation entitled "Recent Developments and Issues in Government Investigations," which provides further insight into the investigation process, as well as the recent trends in this area.

Many contract law violations or perceived violations can result in an agency investigation or audit. Below is a general list of the types of disputes we typically encounter:

- Mischarging/overcharging (false claims)
- Cost/pricing data and defective pricing claims
- Price reduction clause violations

- Poor delivery/product substitution claims
- False statements or certifications of claims
- Conflicts of interest violations
- Procurement Integrity Act violations, such as the "revolving door" restrictions on former government employees
- Anti-Kickback Act violations
- Gifts/gratuities violations

Many of the areas identified above address situations where the government believes it has been overcharged, such as false claims, defective pricing, price reductions clause, and so on. The government also investigates when there are delivery issues, performance issues, product substitution, or if a contractor violated a statutory obligation to refrain from engaging in certain types of activities (e.g., conflicts of interest, kickbacks, gifts, gratuities). When the government questions the amount it has been billed, or believes it has not received the product or service it paid the contractor to provide, or the government believes the company's actions threaten the integrity of the procurement system, companies should expect a government inquiry, audit, or investigation (depending on the severity of the perceived issue) to follow soon thereafter.

Investigations can lead to any number of possible outcomes, but most result in either government declination to pursue the claims/allegations against a contractor or settlement, and sometimes federal court litigation. Most publicly traded federal contractors, however, are not inclined to litigate large-scale cases involving false claims or statutory violations in open court against the government unless all other avenues of resolution are closed. Negative press (or the possibility of an adverse decision by the court) resulting from publicly perceived violations can severely damage a federal contractor's reputation and business with the federal government.

Even when a contractor settles a pending investigation or dispute, or is able to secure a declination from the enforcement authority, the transactional costs and collateral effects associated with achieving a resolution can be substantial. For example, responses to grand jury subpoenas (or inspector general subpoenas) with multiple broad allegations can require production of a huge amount of documentation (both hard copy and electronic). Similarly, bid protests involve the production of an administrative record by the government that can include tens, if not hundreds, of thousands of pages of documents (although more agencies are producing records in electronic format). Claims litigation can also involve document production in the millions of pages that is the equivalent of large commercial litigation.

Performance Issues

Early intervention is essential when working with government agencies on performance issues in contract law. It is advisable to search for a mutually acceptable agreement (business agreement if possible) or develop a corrective action plan that will truly fix the problem (rather than merely put it off). Strategies vary based on the agency, nature of the procurement, and scope of the performance issue. There is no "one size fits all" approach to addressing performance issues. Experience has shown that the best strategies are ones developed collaboratively by the business and legal teams. In addition, it is critical that a lawyer get all the facts from the client to develop the strategy—the good news and the bad news.

Based on my experience, we tend to see the most performance disputes in the following areas:

- Delivery (or failure to deliver)
- Quality or performance issues/product substitution
- Disputes over rates/prices/costs
- Schedule issues (failure to adhere to the schedule in the contract)
- Disputes over the ownership, use, and disclosure of intellectual property
- Warranty issues

If ignored or not adequately addressed, performance disputes can fester and eventually lead to costly audits or investigations. We have helped contractors resolve performance disputes after being retained very late in the game, which can present challenges and issues that go far beyond the mere performance issues that were underlying the dispute.

Researching Claims

The nature of a claim and type of contract involved will often govern the particular areas of inquiry for claim against the government as well as the likelihood of successfully prosecuting a claim against the government. For instance, in an acceleration or delay claim, the project schedule and timelines in the contract are critical data points that need to be fully understood. For claims arising from changes in requirements or added work under fixed price contracts, issues such as government authority and the nature or scope of the changed activity compared to the contract baseline are essential to fully understand. At a minimum, for any type of claim against the government, the starting point always should be the contract's baseline. In other words, what are the specific requirements, schedule, and delivery date in the contract, how did the parties diverge from baselines, and what party bears responsibility (or at least primary responsibility) for that divergence? Using this type of information, we strive to develop a clear, realistic assessment of the likelihood of success of any claim using the contract information early in the claims process.

In addition, here are some other key questions to raise:

- How did the claim arise?
- When does it need to be filed?
- Who are the key company players, and who will certify the claim (if necessary)?
- What type of contract is involved (cost, time and materials, fixed price)?
- Documents, documents, documents. What do we have in writing that supports or undermines the claim?
- Are there any quality of performance issues?
- Are there any subcontractors involved in the claim?
- How does the company plan to prove the amount allegedly owed by the government?
- Is there a written change order from the contracting officer?
- Is there any evidence (preferably written) of government direction/approval (preferably from the contracting officer) of

actions that led to the changes that comprise the basis for the claim?

- Where are the key documents (e.g., copy of the contract, correspondence, etc.)?
- What is the company's ultimate goal (e.g., financial recovery, business resolution, etc.)?
- What other strategic factors are relevant to consider? (Are there future/pending awards? Other performance/compliance issues? Desire to continue to do business with this agency?)
- What are the likely arguments the government will raise against the claim? (Where is the "dirty laundry"? Does the government have counterclaims it might raise against the company?)
- What is the nature of the relationship with the government customer, both historically and presently?

The answers to these questions can help you better understand the likelihood of success of your claim, as well as the strengths and weaknesses inherent in your claim.

Protesting a Contract

When an agency awards a contract to another company, other companies that submitted proposals can challenge the award of the contract through a process known as a bid protest. There are three possible outcomes to a protest: (1) win through a favorable decision, (2) lose through dismissal or an adverse decision, or (3) settlement generally through agency corrective action. However, even once a company wins a bid protest, it could certainly "win the battle but lose the war," in that the typical remedy after a protest is sustained is for the agency to re-compete its requirements. At that stage, the winner of the protest has no guarantee that it will win the business. In fact, it is not unusual for agencies to select the same awardee as before the protest once the agency corrects the errors in the evaluation process that were the subject of the initial protest, but of course there are many factors that will affect any given agency award decision. Clients must also be aware of potential collateral impacts of a protest on its client relationship, which needs to be considered in broader scope of client business objectives. Often a client will decline to protest so as not to upset or disrupt a relationship with the client even though the bid protest rules were set up as the acceptable method to challenge a contract award.

When protesting a contract, we always first assess whether there is a possible business solution that can be proposed to the agency. If not, protests are generally drafted with little information, like a broad complaint based on information and belief, and against very short filing deadlines (e.g., within five or ten days of the date of a required debriefing, or after receipt of information that forms the basis for the protest). However, once a protestor gets access to agency and bid/proposal documentation of the awardee under the bounds of a protective order, we find it is prudent to focus on two or three of the best issues and advance those issues in briefings and a hearing (if one is deemed necessary).

Comprehensive analysis of not only the procurement and evaluation materials, but also the background surrounding the procurement, is essential before initiating a protest, especially on large procurements that are "must wins" for our client. We find that it is invaluable to have the attorneys who will prosecute or defend a potential protest included in the procurement process well before the final award is announced and involved in the post-award debriefing (to the extent one is requested). This participation can include pre-award review of a briefing on the final proposal the client submitted, discussion of evaluation notices (documents that will identify agency perceived deficiencies/weaknesses in a contractor's proposal), and other issues raised by the government during the discussions process, any mid-term or interim evaluations the government provided, and any competitive assessments the client performed. Since, as noted above, protests must be filed very quickly after an award, these briefings can cut down substantially on the amount of time it takes to prepare for a protest and result in a more targeted and persuasive protest filing.

Compliance in Government Contract Law

General Regulations

A wide range of compliance issues may arise when working with federal agencies. Included as Appendix B is a copy of a compliance plan table of contents template that identifies at a high level the areas typically covered by a compliance plan for a government contractor. The federal marketplace is still a highly regulated industry, and much more regulated than the commercial marketplace. It is not unusual to experience the criminalization of what appears to be normal business disputes. Federal investigators have a wide array of weapons at their disposal to address perceived fraud, waste, or abuse by a government contractor. Compliance issues can arise in connection with violations of ethics and integrity statutes or regulations specific to government contracts such as the Anti-Kickback Act, prohibitions on providing gratuities, and the Procurement Integrity Act. Violation of these government contract-specific statutes can result in civil, criminal, or administrative penalties (suspension/debarment), or some combination thereof.

In addition, a wide range of more generally applicable criminal laws also apply to government contractors, such as the Foreign Corrupt Practices Act, bribery laws, antitrust laws, criminal fraud, and many other statutes set forth in Title 18 of the U.S. Code. Included as Appendix C is a June 2007 presentation entitled "Conducting Business in the Federal Marketplace," which discusses potential compliance challenges associated with conducting business with the federal government and how conducting business in the federal marketplace differs significantly from contracting with commercial entities.

Compliance challenges also may arise where a contractor has submitted a claim or statement the government deems to be false or fraudulent. Typically these matters are brought under the False Claims Act or False Statements Act, and can be brought as a criminal or civil matter. In 2008, the Department of Justice recovered $1.34 billion in fraud settlement and judgments under the Civil False Claims Act (an amount that does not include recoveries provided to states), with a total recovery since 1986 of $21 billion dollars. See *The Government Contractor*, Vol. 50, No. 43 ¶ 418 (Nov. 19, 2008).

Finally, the new mandatory disclosure rules (on future, current, and for some past violations) discussed earlier that went into effect on December 12, 2008, will present broad, wide-ranging compliance challenges. The new rule subjects all government contractors to potential suspension/debarment for the knowing failure to report "credible evidence" of criminal violations of procurement-related statutes in Title 18 of the U.S. Code (involving fraud, conflict of interest, bribery, or gratuities), violations of the civil False Claims Act, or substantial overpayments. In addition to the implicit mandatory disclosure required by these new suspension/debarment provisions, the new rule also amends FAR Clause 52.203-13 (which must be inserted in all covered contracts greater than $5 million and more than 120 days in duration) to include similar express mandatory disclosure requirements. The FAR clause requires a company to disclose, in connection with a contract or subcontract, where there is "credible evidence" of criminal violations of procurement-related statutes in Title 18 of the U.S. Code (involving fraud, conflict of interest, bribery, or gratuities) or a violation of the civil False Claims Act. Each of these disclosure obligations affects current contracts, as well as any contracts on which final payment was made to a contractor after December 12, 2005.

In addition, the new FAR rule extends the coverage of portions of FAR Clause 52.203-13 to commercial item contractors and contractors that perform contracts entirely outside the United States, and amplifies the existing requirements for contractors' codes of business ethics and conduct by creating new mandatory minimum requirements for some contractors' internal control systems. A self-described "sea change" from prior voluntary disclosure rules, the new mandatory disclosure rules and enhanced internal controls requirement impose new obligations on a wide range of government contractors, and they demand attention.

Meeting These Requirements

Companies can meet compliance requirements through development and implementation of robust government contract compliance programs that now must include a compliance plan/code of conduct, trainings, and mechanisms to detect and report violations. It is still important, however, that any compliance plan be appropriately tailored to the specific business model of a company (e.g., product versus service, defense versus civilian, commercial item versus non-commercial item, size, and complexity of organization, etc.).

We also have found that the structure of a company and company culture are very important factors to consider when developing a government contract compliance program. Effective government contract compliance programs can be difficult to implement successfully in highly decentralized companies. Many times, structural and reporting changes are necessary in order to implement a successful government contract compliance program for these types of entities, and especially now in light of the new mandatory disclosure rules in the FAR. Similarly, companies that conduct a significant portion of their business in the commercial marketplace tend to have a different culture, which can be challenging when it comes to imposing and enforcing more stringent government contract compliance policies and procedures. A wide variety of practices and activities are acceptable and commonplace in the commercial marketplace, but can be crimes if undertaken with federal customers. The best example involves laws prohibiting most gifts and gratuities, including types that are permissible in the commercial world (e.g., dinners, tickets to sporting events, etc.). Overcoming the endemic culture of such a company can present a significant obstacle to implementing a successful, effective government contract compliance program.

Recommended Policies and Procedures

To ensure compliance with complex government contract statutes and regulations, we recommend that companies doing business with the federal government (whether as a prime contractor or a subcontractor) have a comprehensive standard of business conduct that focuses on government contracts—specific statutory and regulatory requirements. Typically, these standards of conduct are just one piece of a company's government contract compliance program, and may supplement existing company codes of ethics or internal policies. Not only should the government contract standards of conduct cover federal procurement statutory and regulatory requirements, but we recommend that the standards also address issues such as performance standards, submission of information to the government or a prime contractor, record-keeping, violations reporting mechanisms (including hotlines), and discipline for violation of standards. There also should be a process in place to ensure that personnel that work on federal contracts acknowledge receipt of the standards and receive initial training in the areas covered by the standards (as well as refresher training on at least an annual basis, given the fact that the rules and regulations governing conduct in the federal marketplace are ever-changing). Finally, the company should have a process for ensuring its standards of conduct remain up to date, and provide for revision when changes in the law arise in the areas covered by the standards of conduct. There is no doubt that the ability to demonstrate a broad, comprehensive, and holistic approach to compliance can help catch and hopefully mitigate the impact of any violation.

Recommended Compliance Efforts

The steady increase in federal spending and recent high-profile criminal and civil fraud matters involving federal contractors have resulted in closer scrutiny of federal contractors in general. In addition, recent legislation and regulations impose additional compliance and reporting requirements on contractors. Because of these initiatives, it is more critical than ever to ensure that your company's federal procurement policies, practices, and procedures conform to current federal laws and regulations.

We routinely advise contractors on the application of ethics statutes and regulations to their practices in the federal marketplace, and have assisted numerous contractors with establishing and enhancing their ethics and government contract compliance programs to ensure those programs are comprehensive and current. In addition, we have conducted numerous compliance audits for contractors in all industries that provide either products or services to the federal government. These ethics and compliance audits involve assessing current government contract policies, generally through on-site audit and review of relevant documents and interviews of pertinent management and staff; identifying existing ethics/compliance issues, weaknesses, and key areas of risk; proposing and assisting with implementation of recommendations for mitigating known risks; and providing targeted quarterly reviews of specific areas. Typical areas of inquiry in these types of compliance audits include assessment of compliance with:

- Applicable statutory and regulatory requirements
- Prime or subcontract terms and conditions
- The company's code of conduct and related policies/procedures for conducting business in the federal marketplace
- Socioeconomic and reporting requirements

- Security clearance/export compliance procedures (where applicable)
- Internal controls designed to ensure overall compliance with government contracting requirements (including but not limited to training programs, violation detection mechanisms, management involvement/"tone at the top," and disciplinary and corrective actions for violations).

Where a compliance audit has been initiated in connection with, or in response to, a government investigation, we also work with the company to develop and implement the corrective action plans and other remedial measures, critical to mitigating the risk of suspension or debarment based on any alleged misconduct and preventing future occurrences of similar prohibited conduct.

Finally, it is important not the understate the impact of the new FAR rule issued on November 12, 2008, in terms of the additional compliance requirements it will impose on federal contractors. The new FAR rule on business ethics compliance programs and mandatory disclosure will force contractors to take immediate steps to ensure that their current compliance program is consistent with the new requirements. While we believe current compliance programs for large contractors likely will cover many of the areas addressed in the new rule, all contractors must confirm that their compliance program satisfies the following new requirements imposed by the final rule. Below are some high-level recommendations on steps contractors should consider taking in response to the new FAR rule:

- **Mandatory disclosure:** The new rule subjects all government contractors to potential suspension/debarment for the knowing failure to report "credible evidence" of criminal violations of procurement-related statutes in Title 18 of the U.S. Code (involving fraud, conflict of interest, bribery, or gratuities), violations of the civil False Claims Act, or substantial overpayments. In addition to the implicit mandatory disclosure required by these new suspension/debarment provisions, the new rule also amends FAR Clause 52.203-13 (which must be inserted in all covered contracts greater than $5 million and more than 120 days in duration) to include similar express mandatory disclosure requirements. The

FAR clause requires a company to disclose, in connection with a contract or subcontract, where there is "credible evidence" of a violation of a federal criminal law involving fraud, conflict of interest, bribery, or gratuity violations, or a violation of the civil False Claims Act. Each of these disclosure obligations affect current contracts, as well as any contracts on which final payment was made to a company after December 12, 2005. Identified below are additional compliance/control structures contractors may want to consider in order to ensure compliance with the new FAR rule's broad mandatory disclosure requirements:

- We recommend that contractors consider designating collection points in each business unit to collect and review information that may constitute a violation. Any such review that is conducted also should be documented in a written report.
- Consider designating a defined "funnel point" where the collection points from the business units will report any information of a possible violation. Consider also whether to make this funnel point person responsible for reporting any possible violations to upper management.
- Consider implementing a system to coordinate and review all possible violations to determine if the company has credible evidence of a violation and is therefore required to disclose that evidence to the government or an agency inspector general. In the event the company becomes aware of a possible violation and, upon investigation, determines it lacks credible evidence of the violation and elects not to disclose to the government, the company should implement procedures to ensure that the decision is thoroughly documented in the event the decision is later questioned/challenged as a knowing failure to report.
- Consider implementing a system to provide some degree of oversight of subcontractors to detect subcontractor violations. Of particular note, there is also a new requirement for companies to provide ethics and compliance training to subcontractors "as appropriate," which may include circumstances in which a subcontractor

lacks a robust compliance plan program and/or sufficient training program.

- Consider the need to make any "catch-up" disclosures of known violations or overpayments on current contracts, or any for which final payment was made within the last three years. Previously unreported violations of criminal conduct involving fraud, conflict of interest, bribery, gratuities, violations of the False Claims Act, or significant overpayments on these contracts could subject a company to suspension/debarment if they are not properly reported to the government.
- Consider the need to refresh any disclosures that have already been made to the government if those disclosures were not made directly to an agency inspector general. The revised FAR Clause 52.203-13 will require disclosures of criminal conduct involving fraud, conflict of interest, bribery, gratuities, and violations of the civil False Claims Act to be reported directly to the cognizant inspector general (with a copy to the contracting officer). Prior disclosures made to other government officials (i.e., the contracting officer or the Department of Justice) on current contracts or those closed after December 12, 2005, may need to redirected to the inspector general.

- **Ongoing business ethics and awareness compliance program and internal controls system:** The new FAR rule also requires contractors with a covered contract to have a compliance program in place that meets the following requirements:

  - Reasonable efforts not to include an individual as a principal, whom due diligence would have exposed as having engaged in conduct that is in conflict with the contractor's code of business ethics and conduct.

    - "Principal" means an officer, director, owner, partner, or a person having primary management or supervisory responsibilities within a business entity (e.g., general manager, plant manager, head of a subsidiary, division, or business segment). FAR 2.101(b)(2).

- Past criminal behavior of any type, even criminal behavior unrelated to contracting, calls into question whether the individual has integrity and is a proper role model for company staff. Note, however, that this is not a mandate to fire the individual, but to determine whether the individual is currently trustworthy to serve as a principal of the company.

- Assignment of responsibility at a sufficiently high level and adequate resources to ensure effectiveness of the ethics awareness and compliance program and internal control system
- Periodic reviews of practices, procedures, policies, and internal controls, including monitoring and auditing to detect criminal conduct, evaluation of effectiveness of programs, and assessment of the risk of criminal conduct and changes to internal programs to address those risks
- Internal reporting mechanism (hotline) that allows anonymity or confidentiality
- Disciplinary action for improper conduct or for failing to take reasonable steps to prevent or detect improper conduct
- "Full cooperation" (as defined in the final rule) with any government agencies responsible for audits, investigations, or corrective actions

In summary, while it remains to be seen how government enforcement authorities (particularly agency inspector generals) interpret the new FAR rule, they and other broad government enforcement activities mandate heightened awareness in the area of government contract compliance.

Closing Advice

Early in my career, I was told to be aware that the government contract bar is a small one where the agency lawyer who was your adversary last week where you represented a protester may be your co-counsel on a protest the next week. Reputation in this industry is absolutely critical, and as an advocate, it is my job to protect and preserve it for our clients. Therefore, the "slash and burn" strategies employed on many commercial litigation matters can be a recipe for disaster for most government contract matters. Instead, experience has taught me that frank, yet respectful discussions with agency representatives can yield better results than immediate resort to adversarial tactics. To that end and in all dealings with federal agency representatives, I always strive to ensure that lines of communication are opened early with agency counsel and remain open, even when a matter does not move at the optimal pace or where positions taken by an agency may seem at first glance untenable. When faced with such situations, my advice is always to take a deep breath, put yourself in the agency's position, and think about how best to resolve the area in dispute rather than immediately report to adversarial skirmishes.

Eric W. Leonard is a partner at Wiley Rein LLP (formerly known as Wiley, Rein & Fielding LLP), and he has been assisting federal contractors as part of Wiley Rein's thirty-person government contracts practice since 1997. The firm represents a wide spectrum of federal contractors in virtually all industries, including defense and aerospace, information technology, professional services, telecommunications, health care, and construction services that conduct business with the federal government. Mr. Leonard has represented both large and small contractors in government contract matters before federal agencies (including the Department of Justice and agency inspector general offices), the Government Accountability Office, and the U.S. Court of Federal Claims. He has experience in a wide range of government contract areas, including bid protest litigation at the Government Accountability Office and Court of Federal Claims, government contract compliance issues (including compliance with federal labor initiatives such as the Service Contract Act, the Davis Bacon Act, and Equal Employment Opportunity obligations), federal investigation and subpoena matters (including procurement fraud and qui tam *litigation), contract negotiation, and preparation of claims. He is also a vice chair of the American Bar Association's public contracts, procurement, and fraud committee, and he is a frequent lecturer in the areas of government contract compliance and service contracting.*

Acknowledgment: *Special thanks to Jon Burd for his invaluable assistance.*

Government Contracts Law and Intellectual Property Rights

William C. Bergmann

Partner

Baker Hostetler LLP

Introduction

Intellectual property rights are increasingly important to both small and large companies in the global economy, particularly those companies engaged in high-technology areas. For some companies, their intellectual property rights (patents, trademarks, copyrights, and trade secrets) are their most valuable assets. For companies working with government agencies, this focus is no less important. The government funds a large amount of research and development work in the United States. It further funds a large amount of contract work that results in the first application of a particular technology in a commercialized product, for use by the government or private sector.

A government contract represents an opportunity for a company to develop this technology with government funding while retaining a substantial amount of the intellectual property rights for itself. To retain as many intellectual property rights as possible, however, a government contractor must be aware of, and be careful to abide by, the many statutes and regulations dealing with intellectual property involved with government procurement. Failure to observe these statutes and regulations may result in a company losing its intellectual property rights.

It is also important for a government contractor to put itself in position to defend itself against charges of infringement that may occur because of its government contract work. Since many government contracts involve the development and manufacture of large and complex systems, it is not unusual for an owner of intellectual property rights (particularly patent rights) to allege that the performance of a government contract will result in the infringement of those rights. Under 28 U.S.C. § 1498(a) and (b), and 15 U.S.C. § 1122, a patent, copyright, or trademark holder can sue the United States for infringement committed by the government or its contractors during the performance of government contract work.

If the government is sued for infringement, contractors and subcontractors may in turn be liable to indemnify the government for any damages suffered because of the infringement allegations. In view of this, government contractors should be aware of the relevant statutory and Federal Acquisition Regulation (FAR) provisions governing intellectual property disputes. In addition, a government contractor may find it necessary to enforce its own intellectual property rights against the government and/or other government contractors, should a competitor be awarded a contract that may result in a violation of a company's intellectual property rights. For example, the government may award a contract to a competitor even though the competitor will necessarily infringe a company's patent rights during the performance of the contract. If this occurs, the company's only recourse is to sue the United States in the Court of Federal Claims for patent infringement.

Finally, a government contractor should be careful to address the disposition of intellectual property rights when entering into so-called "teaming agreements" with other contractors in order to bid on government contracts as a team. During the performance of a government contract, the contractors may jointly invent things, create computer software, or develop a Web site, for example. The question of who will ultimately own this intellectual property should be addressed in the teaming agreement before potential disputes arise.

The Disposition of Intellectual Property Rights Involved in Government Contracts

The creation of intellectual property rights during the performance of work funded by the federal government can occur whenever a contractor employee invents or authors something while working on a government contract. The rights to that invention or work will typically be governed by statute and/or regulation. The government contracting arena relating to the development of new technology is vast and diverse, encompassing, for example, university grants, small business development contracts, and billion-dollar programs relating to major weapons systems. Given the subject matter of these contracts, it is therefore likely that there will be new intellectual property created during the performance of work on them.

Historically there has been a hodge-podge of statutes and regulations governing the disposition of intellectual property rights created during the performance of work funded by the government. In general—with many caveats—it has been the policy of the federal government to allow contractors to keep ownership rights in inventions made with federal funding while retaining a non-exclusive, paid-up license to practice the invention on behalf of the United States. See Presidential Memorandum to the Heads of Executive Departments and Agencies on Government Patent Policy issued February 18, 1983; Executive Order 12591 (Apr. 10, 1987), 52 FR 13414, 3 CFR, 1987 Comp., p. 220. Part of the reason behind this policy is the theory that the contractor is in a better position to commercialize an invention than the federal government. The non-exclusive license obtained by the government in such instances inures to the benefit of other government contractors performing work on behalf of the government. Some of the more important statutes and regulations governing the disposition of intellectual property rights as they relate to government contracts will be discussed below.

Patent Rights in Inventions Made with Federal Funding for Small Businesses and Non-Profit Organizations in Research and Development Contracts

The policy of the federal government with respect to the disposition of invention rights made with federal funding for small businesses and non-profit organizations has been made relatively uniform and has been codified at Chapter 18 of Title 35 (35 U.S.C. §§ 200–212). The highlights of this chapter are:

- "Subject inventions" are defined as "any invention of the contractor conceived or first actually reduced to practice in the performance of work under a funding agreement." (35 U.S.C. § 201(e))
- Non-profit organizations and small businesses may elect to retain title to subject inventions, provided that the funding agreement may provide otherwise in certain circumstances. (35 U.S.C. § 202(a))
- "Funding agreement" is defined broadly as any contract, grant, or cooperative agreement entered into between any federal agency and the contractor for the performance of experimental, developmental, or research work. (35 U.S.C. § 201(b))
- The government retains a non-exclusive, non-transferable, irrevocable, paid-up license to practice the invention for or on behalf of the United States throughout the world. (35 U.S.C. § 202(c)(4))

- The contractor must disclose the existence of each "subject invention" to the government, elect to take title to the invention, and prosecute the patent application for the invention. Failure to do so may result in title to the invention vesting with the government. (35 U.S.C. § 202(c))
- The funding agreement may require the contractor to report on the real-world utilization of the invention. (35 U.S.C. § 202(c)(5))
- The federal government retains "march-in" rights to force the contractor to grant a non-exclusive or exclusive license to others in a particular field of use if the contractor is not taking reasonable steps to achieve the practical application of the invention in the field of use or for public health or safety reasons. (35 U.S.C. § 203(a))
- Preferences are made for U.S. industries throughout Chapter 18, for example, in the granting title to invention rights (§ 202(a)(i)), the manufacture of subject inventions (§ 204), and in the licensing of inventions owned by the federal government (§ 209(b)).

Prior to the enactment of Chapter 18, both federal agencies and specialized areas of technology could have their own different rules regarding the disposition of rights in inventions developed with federal funding. Section 210 of Title 35 states that the provisions of Chapter 18 take precedence over any other conflicting statute, and it specifically lists twenty-one different statutes over which it takes precedence. Section 210 even goes so far as to state that it takes precedence over *future* acts, unless the future act specifically provides that Chapter 18 does not apply.

Many of the statutes that are now potentially superseded by Chapter 18 have not been amended to reflect this, and a practitioner confronted with a potentially conflicting statute should always be careful to research the appropriate controlling law in view of § 210. For example, § 210(1) lists a statute codified at 7 U.S.C. § 427i(a) that discusses the disposition of rights in inventions made with funding pursuant to Department of Agriculture contracts. That statute reads, in part: "Any contracts made pursuant to this authority shall contain requirements making the results of research and investigations available to the public through dedication, assignment to the Government, or such other means as the Secretary shall determine." Since this disposition of rights is contrary to the provisions of Chapter 18, the provisions of Chapter 18 should be controlling, at least with respect to small businesses and non-profit entities.

Patent Rights in Inventions Made with Federal Funding for All Other Contracts and Contractors

In 1983, President Reagan extended the statutory provisions governing the disposition of invention rights for small businesses and non-profit organizations found at 35 U.S.C. §§ 200-212 (formerly Chapter 38) to all other government contractors in a Presidential Memorandum to the Heads of Executive Departments and Agencies on Government Patent Policy dated February 18, 1983:

> To the extent permitted by law, agency policy with respect to the disposition of any invention made in the performance of a federally-funded research and development contract, grant or cooperative agreement award shall be the same or substantially the same as applied to small business firms and non-profit organizations under Chapter 38 of Title 35 of the United States Code.

This memorandum had the effect of granting title to inventions made with federal funding to all contractors regardless of size, but like 35 U.S.C. §§ 200-212, it only applied to a "federally funded research and development contract, grant or cooperative agreement." This limitation was apparently removed by Executive Order No. 12591, dated April 10, 1987, which states at Section 1(b)(4) that the head of each executive department and agency shall, within overall funding allocations and to the extent permitted by law:

> Promote the commercialization, in accord with my Memorandum to the Heads of Executive Departments and Agencies of February 18, 1983, of patentable results of federally funded research by granting to all contractors, regardless of size, the title to patents made in whole or in part with federal funds, in exchange for royalty-free use by or on behalf of the government.

Therefore, in general, title to inventions made with federal funding vest in the contractor, with the government taking a royalty-free license for use of the invention by or on behalf of the government. The language "by or on behalf of the government" means the government's contractors and subcontractors are also included within the scope of the government's license, as long as the work they are performing is within the scope of their government contract.

Copyright and Trademark Rights Relating to Government Contracts

As a general rule, the ownership of copyrighted works created with federal funding will be governed by the contractual provisions of the government contract under which the work was created. One statute of interest, however, is 17 U.S.C. § 105. Under this statute, the U.S. government cannot obtain copyright protection for any work created by the U.S. government, but can obtain ownership of a copyrighted work transferred to it by assignment:

> Copyright protection under this title is not available for any work of the United States Government, but the United States Government is not precluded from receiving and holding copyrights transferred to it by assignment, bequest, or otherwise.
>
> 17 U.S.C. § 105.

When a government agency wants to obtain ownership of a copyrighted work, it will often contract the work out so it can then achieve ownership of a copyrighted work by assignment, as permitted under § 105. In this instance, the agency will insert the appropriate FAR clause, discussed below, into the contract between itself and the contractor hired to create the work. This clause will obligate the contractor to assign any copyrighted works created during the performance of the contract over to the government.

Unlike copyrights, the U.S. government can create its own trademarks and own them. Ownership of trademark rights created during the performance of a government contract is usually not an issue, however, since it occurs infrequently. A contractor typically may use its preexisting trademarks during the performance of a government contract without concerns that the government will somehow obtain ownership rights in those trademarks. In the event that a government contract specifically calls for the creation of a design or logo that is intended to serve as a trademark for the government, the contract should contain a clause specifying that ownership rights of any trademark created during the performance of the contract belong to the government.

FAR Clauses and Practice Tips

The policy of the federal government with respect to the ownership of intellectual property rights developed during the performance of government contracts is put into practice by the FAR. The FAR is found in Chapter 1 of Volume 48 of the Code of Federal Regulations, and is the regulation that applies to almost all government procurement. Conceptually the FAR can be said to be divided into two portions. The first portion consists of a narrative that explains government policies and contracting procedures, and directs the contracting officer to apply certain rules and insert certain clauses into a government contract depending upon the specific situation. This portion is found in Chapter 1, Parts 1 through 51. The second portion of the FAR is the actual contract clauses themselves, found in Part 52 of Chapter 1.

The FAR contract clauses are akin to boilerplate clauses found in private contracts, and the language of them cannot be negotiated by a contractor. Often the contract clauses implement important statutory or other policy directives of Congress and the president, and contracting officers are not free to change their language. On occasion, however, their insertion into a particular contract is discretionary. See, e.g., FAR 27.303(e)(1). In these instances, a contractor may be able to negotiate whether a particular clause will be inserted into a contract.

In addition, many of the clauses have different versions. The contracting officer is supposed to select the appropriate version to use, depending upon the guidance provided in the FAR. In some instances, a contractor may be able to persuade a contracting officer that the applicable rules dictate that one particular version of a clause should be used rather than the version selected by the contracting officer, or argue that the clause should not be included at all. For example, FAR 27.201-2(c) specifies that a particular version of the patent indemnity clause requiring the contractor to indemnify the government for patent infringement should be included in contracts if "the clause would be consistent with commercial practice." This phrase leaves room for interpretation by the contracting officer, and an objection to its inclusion by the contractor may be possible.

With respect to intellectual property rights, Chapter 1, Part 27, contains the policies and procedures to be followed by the contracting officer relating to patents, rights in data, and copyrights. The actual contract clauses relating to intellectual property are in general found at Part 52.227. A summary of the more significant clauses relating to patent, copyright, and data rights follows.

Significant FAR Clauses Relating to Patent, Copyright, and Data Rights

- 52.227-11 and 52.227-12 Patent Rights—Retention by the Contractor. These clauses incorporate the statutory provisions of 35 U.S.C. §§ 200-212 discussed above and grant title in subject inventions to the contractor, subject to several conditions. The contracting officer will use either 52.227-11 (short form) or 52.227-12 (long form) as is appropriate.
- 52.227-13 Patent Rights—Acquisition by the Government. This clause is infrequently used, but if present, it requires the contractor to assign patent rights in subject inventions to the government.
- 52.227-14 Rights in Data—General. This is the main contract clause that delineates the respective rights of the contractor and the government in data and software that preexists the performance of contract work, and delineates the rights in data and software that is created during the performance of the contract. A contracting officer can select from five alternate clauses, depending upon the specific circumstances of the contract. The clauses allocate data rights between the contractor and the government to varying degrees.

The policy of the government with respect to rights in data and software is expressed at FAR 27.402. This includes any copyrights in the data or software. In general, the government recognizes that both parties to a government contract have an interest in both data and software rights. The interest of both parties exists for data and software that exists before the contract is entered into, and for data and software that is created during the performance of the contract. The government has an interest in acquiring rights in both data and software so that it may freely use them after the conclusion of the contract. At the same time, the government recognizes that the contractor may have a legitimate proprietary interest in protecting its data and software. The contracting officer is therefore instructed to balance these two interests in determining which of the five alternate clauses of FAR 52.227-14 to incorporate into the contract. FAR 52.227-15 through 23 are additional data rights clauses that can be used in particular circumstances to delineate the allocation of data and software rights among the contracting parties.

Conception and Actual Reduction to Practice

By both statute and regulation, the government takes rights in any "subject invention" under a federally funded contract. A subject invention is defined under 35 U.S.C. § 201(e) as "any invention of the contractor conceived or first actually reduced to practice in the performance of work under a funding agreement." An actual reduction to practice of an invention can be loosely thought of as the first successful testing of the invention, whereas a constructive reduction to practice can occur when an inventor files a patent application for the invention. An inventor is typically given credit in patent law for conceiving of an idea and then reducing it to practice, even if the reduction to practice is done constructively by filing a patent application.

The phrase giving the government rights in inventions "conceived or first *actually* reduced to practice in the performance of work under a funding agreement" is therefore broader than many contractors fully appreciate. Under government contracting law, the government obtains rights in an invention that is first "actually" reduced to practice during the performance of a government contract, regardless of whether the inventor has already applied for a patent on the invention prior to entering into a government contract.

This policy is seen as a balancing of equities. The government often contributes vast sums of money to complex projects that would be difficult for a private entity to undertake (e.g., the construction and launching of satellites, aircraft carriers, or advanced jet fighters). In exchange for receiving a large contract to undertake a complex project, a government contractor must give the government a non-exclusive, royalty-free license in any invention that is first "actually" reduced to practice during the course of the contract. The contractor retains the rights in the invention for non-government use, and is free to commercialize the invention for private-sector use.

Practice Tips

- Actual Reduction to Practice

For inventions that can be actually reduced to practice without significant effort, the contractor should construct an experimental model or prototype, and reduce the invention to practice before entering into a government contract so it retains all rights to the invention.

- Document Work Done Before Entering Into Contract

Contractors should be careful to document the work that was performed towards conception and actual reduction to practice of inventions prior to entering into government contracts. Many government contracts call for a report to be issued by the contractor at the conclusion of the contract detailing the progress that was made in constructing and testing any devices built during the contract. This will evidence that any inventions involved with the project were actually reduced to practice during the contract. If the contractor wishes to show this was not the "first" actual reduction to practice, the contractor should meticulously document any work done before entering into the government contract to show that the inventions were first actually reduced to practice beforehand.

Contractors can also make it clear in requests for proposals that they intend to rely on preexisting technology in the performance of contract work, and describe in detail the preexisting technology. For example, a contractor can state that they intend to use the technology described in a particular patent or patent application during the course of the contract work, and, preferably, indicate that a working prototype of the technology already exists. This negates any questions about whether the contractor was in possession of the idea before contract work begins.

- Ensure Key Contract Clauses Are Incorporated Into Subcontracts

It is always good practice to make sure any flow-down clauses that are required to be in subcontracts are actually present. For example, FAR 52.203-13(b) requires contractors and subcontractors to follow certain ethical guidelines, and a prime contractor would always want to make sure subcontractors are explicitly given notice of these requirements. In addition, careful consideration should be given to incorporating other prime contract clauses into a subcontract so the prime contractor's rights are not negatively affected.

This general advice applies to the FAR clauses associated with patent and data rights as well. For example, the applicable FAR clauses call for subject inventions to be identified and reported to the contracting agency. If this is not done, the government can take title to subject inventions. During the contract work, it may not be evident at first whether the prime contractor, a subcontractor, or both invented something. To avoid any disputes in this area, it is better to have both the prime and the subcontractor aware of the reporting requirement so a subject invention is not neglected to be reported because each contractor felt it was the other's duty to report it.

- Develop a Checklist

Contractors should consider developing a checklist of tasks that must be accomplished in order to comply with the statutory and FAR requirements relating to invention rights to make sure these rights are not lost. Items a contractor must take action on include (1) timely reporting of subject inventions, (2) electing title to subject inventions, (3) filing for patents on subject inventions or notifying agencies of a decision not to file for patents, (4) acknowledging government support and the government's license in the invention, (5) submitting annual utilization reports, and (6) ensuring that any royalties received for the utilization of subject inventions comply with applicable regulations.

- Review FAR Provisions and Determine if More Favorable Clauses Can Be Substituted

As was discussed above, the actual language of the FAR clauses cannot be negotiated. The decision whether to include a clause or one of its alternatives may be discretionary or subject to reasonable interpretation, however, and a contractor should review the FAR to make sure the contracting officer has selected the appropriate clause based on the facts of the particular contract being contemplated.

Claims against the Federal Government and Its Contractors for Patent, Copyright, and Trademark Infringement

Even seasoned practitioners are often surprised to learn that the federal government can be sued for patent, copyright, and trademark infringement. Under 28 U.S.C. §§ 1498(a) and (b), the government can be sued in the Court of Federal Claims for patent and copyright infringement, and under 15 U.S.C. § 1122, the government can be sued in district court for trademark infringement. The ability to sue the government for patent infringement has existed for almost 100 years, while the statute permitting the government to be sued for trademark infringement is relatively recent.

Statutory Framework and Differences between Claims against the Government and Claims against Private Parties for Infringement

A lawsuit against the government for patent, copyright, or trademark infringement is analogous to a suit against a private party, but has critical differences that are important to government contractors. First, the right to sue the government is based upon a waiver of sovereign immunity. With regards to patent and copyright claims, the waiver of immunity is contained within the statutory language of 28 U.S.C. § 1498, and this language specifies several differences between a § 1498 action and an action for patent infringement under Title 35, or one for copyright infringement under Title 17. Technically the government does not "infringe" patents and copyrights, but is said to commit "unauthorized use or manufacture." Case law and even the FAR provisions, however, often refer to the government as committing "infringement," and the legal elements required to prove infringement are the same.

An action for patent and copyright infringement against the government may only be brought in the Court of Federal Claims in Washington, D.C., as is specified by § 1498(a) for patent actions:

> Whenever an invention described in and covered by a patent of the United States is used or manufactured by or for the United States without license of the owner thereof or lawful right to use or manufacture the same, the owner's remedy shall be by action against the United States in the United States Court of Federal Claims for the recovery of his reasonable and entire compensation for such use and manufacture.

Section 1498(b) has similar language concerning claims against the government for copyright infringement. While the body of case law concerning claims for copyright infringement against the government is not as developed as the law concerning claims for patent infringement, most of the law with respect to patent infringement claims should be analogously applicable to claims for copyright infringement, since the statutory basis for the claims is similar.

Because a claim against the government for unauthorized use of patents and copyrights is said to be a waiver of sovereign immunity, and waivers of sovereign immunity are to be construed narrowly, many of the remedies available to a patentee and copyright holder in an action against a private party are not available against the government. For example, the government cannot be enjoined from further unauthorized use. *Motorola, Inc. v. United States*, 729 F.2d 765, 768 n.3 (Fed. Cir. 1984). The only remedy available to the patent or copyright holder is damages in the form of "reasonable and entire compensation." Further, the government cannot be said to "willfully" infringe or be subject to enhanced damages and attorneys' fees because its use is permitted as a sovereign, and the statutory waiver of immunity does not encompass enhanced damages for willful infringement. Id. Nor can the government be liable for induced or contributory infringement. Id. While the government can, in theory, be liable for lost profits, it is difficult for a patent or copyright holder to obtain this measure of damages in practice.

Of critical important to government contractors is language in § 1498 that states that work performed by government contractors and subcontractors during the course of the contract is considered as "use or manufacture" by the government itself:

> For the purposes of this section, the use or manufacture of an invention described in and covered by a patent of the United States by a contractor, a subcontractor, or any person, firm, or corporation for the Government and with the authorization or consent of the Government, shall be construed as use or manufacture for the United States.

Because of this provision, the government effectively assumes liability for any infringing acts committed by its contractors or subcontractors occurring during the performance of government contract work. Further, government contractors cannot be enjoined from their contract work, cannot be found liable for willful infringement or enhanced damages because of their contract work, and cannot be found liable for induced or contributory infringement because of their contract work.

Any action alleging infringement by a government contractor for work performed during the course of a government contract must be brought against the United States in the Court of Federal Claims, and any judgments for monetary damages will be against the United States, not the contractor. An action against a contractor in district court may be dismissed if the contractor pleads that its work is being performed "by or for the government" as an affirmative defense. *Crater Corp. v. Lucent Technologies, Inc.* 255 F.3d 1361, 1369 (Fed. Cir. 2001). Since the government rarely manufactures items itself, almost all Court of Federal Claims actions for infringement involve an accused product or service that was sold to the government by a government contractor. The United States and all of its agencies are represented by the Department of Justice in § 1498 actions.

Indemnification Obligations of Contractors and Participation in Proceedings

By contract, the government may require its contractors to indemnify the government for patent, trademark, and copyright infringement damages suffered by the government due to infringing acts committed by the contractor during the course of government contract work. For example, FAR 52.212-4 and FAR 52.227-3 are two contract provisions that obligate the contractor to indemnify the government for infringement damages. In this instance, a contractor may intervene in the Court of Federal Claims action to protect its interests. See *Carrier Corp. v. United States,* 209 Ct.Cl. 267 (1976); *Rockwell Int'l Corp. v. United States*, 31 Fed. Cl. 536 (1994).

Even if a contractor is not obligated to indemnify the government, it may wish to intervene in a Court of Federal Claims action to protect its interests. No contractor wants a finding by a court that their product infringes a patent or copyright, particularly if they intend to sell more of this product to the government or develop a commercial market for the product. In the event that the contractor develops a commercial version of the product (or already has one) for non-government sales, the patent or copyright holder would be able to sue the contractor directly for commercial sales in district court and argue that the Court of Federal Claims finding of infringement should be adopted by the district court.

Whether by intervening as a party or not, the contractor will invariably be participating in the Court of Federal Claims proceeding as a source of evidence, since it most likely has documents and witnesses with knowledge of the accused product. FAR 52.227-2, if present, actually requires the contractor to assist the government in the defense of the action. For these reasons, a contractor may want to join the action as a party so it may have all of the rights of a party (e.g., ability to take discovery, file briefs, and participate in the proceedings to the extent that it desires), rather than be subject to the negatives of litigation (e.g., discovery demands) without any of the benefits. Since the government is also a customer of the contractor, the contractor will want to support the government in the defense of the action for business reasons as well.

Significant FAR Clauses Relating to Intellectual Property Litigation

- 52.227-1 Authorization and Consent. Insertion of this clause is important to the contractor because in it the government explicitly authorizes and consents to the use and manufacture of any invention covered by a U.S. patent during the performance of the contract. The clause confirms that the work done by the contractor and by any subcontractor is done on behalf of the government, and that any infringement action is against the government pursuant to 28 U.S.C. § 1498 and not against the contractor. This clause must be included within in all subcontracts.

- 52.227-2 Notice and Assistance Regarding Patent and Copyright Infringement. This clause obligates the contractor to notify the government of any allegations of patent or copyright infringement arising during the performance of the contract, and obligates the contractor to assist the government in defending against any infringement claims. The government will pay for the cost of assisting in the defense of a claim, unless an indemnification clause is also included in the contract. This clause must be included within all subcontracts.
- 52.227-3 Patent Indemnity. This clause obligates the contractor to indemnify the government against liability for infringement of any U.S. patent occurring during the performance of the contract. The contractor must be given notice of the action alleging infringement and be allowed to participate in the defense, however.
- 52.212-4 Contract Terms and Conditions—Commercial Items. This is a commonly used clause in government procurement that incorporates several commercial terms. Paragraph (h) of this clause obligates the contractor to indemnify the government against any liability for patent, trademark, and copyright infringement arising out of the performance of the contract.

In general, the guidelines to the contracting officer instruct the officer to insert an indemnity provision into a contract when the contract is for a commercial item. For research and development contracts, the indemnity clause is typically not inserted. The policy behind this approach is the belief that the government should not be liable for infringement damages when it is merely procuring commercial items in much the same way as a private party would. If the government contractor is engaging in research and development work, however, the contractor should be allowed the freedom to research, design, and develop the best possible deliverable under the contract without regard to infringement concerns.

It is also worth noting that while the authorization, consent, notice, and assistance clauses are "flow-down" clauses that must be included in any subcontract, the indemnity provisions are not. Therefore, a contractor should be careful to include an indemnity provision in any subcontract in which the main contract includes such a provision.

Government Procurement Policy Reflected in the Herbert Cooper *Decision*

One of the quirks of government procurement policy with respect to intellectual property rights is the fact that the government is supposed to procure items "without regard to possible infringement" of intellectual property rights held by others. This policy was expressed by the comptroller general in the *Herbert Cooper* decision, 38 Comp. Gen. 276, B- 136916, 1958 CPD P 98, 1958 WL 1753 (Comp.Gen.). In this decision, the comptroller general was asked by the secretary of the Air Force whether to consider the patent rights of others when awarding a contract to the low bidder, the Herbert Cooper Company. The comptroller general held:

> In a procurement by formal advertising involving a patented article and including in the invitation the patent consent and indemnity clauses, an award is required to be made to the lowest bidder meeting the specifications without regard to possible patent infringement, and even though some of the other bidders hold patents or licenses for the article it would be improper to reject all bids and negotiate with the patent holders or licensees.

The effect of this decision, still binding upon agencies today, is that an agency is not supposed to consider whether an award of a contract to the winning bidder will infringe a patent (or presumably copyright or trademark) held by others as long as the contract has an indemnification clause within it. The policy behind this is the government's desire to shift the burden of evaluating the strength and likelihood of any infringement allegations to the contract bidders, and allow them to adjust their bids accordingly based upon their perceived risk of indemnification. After all bids are received, the award of the contract is then made without regard to patent rights.

Practice Tips

In summary, when entering into a government contract, and faced with potential litigation over your government sales, it is important to follow these key practice tips:

- Make sure flow-down clauses are incorporated into subcontracts (i.e., include authorization and consent, notice and assistance, and indemnification flow-through clauses to any subcontractor).
- Determine whether to have the Department of Justice represent you or to intervene in the case if the government is sued over goods or services you have supplied. Either way, it is to your advantage to cooperate with the Department of Justice and the government agency practicing the accused device, since your relationship is that of co-defendants and they are your customer.
- Determine whether there is a commercial market for your intellectual property apart from the government market. If there is a commercial market, intervention in the case to protect your rights may be preferable to make sure your interests (as opposed to the government's interests) are represented.
- Plead lack of jurisdiction over a case or portion of a case that deals with government sales if sued in district court as an affirmative defense. This will remove the action to the Court of Federal Claims where a patentee has fewer rights, and may avoid liability for the contractor if there is no indemnification clause in the government contract.
- Notify the government of patent rights that may be involved in a new government contract. Under *Herbert Cooper*, a contracting agency will not consider those rights in evaluating bids but should insert an indemnification clause into the contract, and competitors must consider it when submitting competing bids. The cost of indemnifying the government for patent infringement should, in theory, discourage bidders and raise the cost of their bids.

Teaming Agreements

Teaming agreements are agreements entered into by prime contractors and subcontractors when teaming up to respond to a government request for proposal or other offer for solicitation. The government procures many large-scale items (e.g., ballistic missiles, nuclear submarines, tanks) that would be impossible for a single contractor to bid on. Contractors find it necessary or advantageous to team up with each other when bidding on even medium- or small-scale items or services being procured by the government.

Different contractors bring different strengths to the table, and by teaming up the contractors can present a stronger proposal to the government than if they had bid on the project alone. Many factors are involved in evaluating a government contract award that would not normally be present in a typical commercial contract. For example, being a small or minority-owned business, or being located in a certain geographical or congressional district, may formally or informally influence the outcome of a particular award. Different team members can satisfy certain criteria, and the resulting bid will be stronger.

The teaming agreement defines the rights and roles of the parties during the bidding process, and thereafter should the team be awarded the contract. Important parts of any teaming agreement are the provisions defining the intellectual property rights of the team members. Care should be taken to allocate intellectual property rights between parties and to document who had developed what prior to entering into a teaming agreement. The teaming agreement should specifically address the question of how any intellectual property rights generated during the performance of the contract work will be allocated. Team members should take care to document instances in which intellectual property has been developed prior to entering into a teaming agreement to avoid disputes later on.

For example, if a contract calls for the development of a Web site for the government, the team members bidding on the contract should specify in the teaming agreement what existing software and Web content they intend to use in the performance of the contract, and who owns it. In addition, if the government contract allows the contractors to retain ownership rights in the Web site, the teaming agreement should also specify which party or parties to the teaming agreement would own those rights after the Web site has been developed.

Conclusion

Intellectual property rights are an important part of most government contracts. The contractor often has the opportunity to develop intellectual property for its own benefit, while being funded by the federal government. Government policy encourages this, with the provision that the government usually takes a non-exclusive license in the intellectual property being developed. Contractors must pay close attention to the contracting provisions involved, however, to ensure they comply with regulations governing the disposition of intellectual property rights. In addition, contractors must be aware of the relevant provisions relating to infringement actions against the government based on work performed by the contractor in order to minimize any liability they may have associated with this work.

William C. Bergmann is a partner with Baker Hostetler LLP. He worked as a trial and appellate attorney for twelve years at the U.S. Department of Justice, specializing in patent, trademark, copyright, and government contract litigation. He is admitted to practice before the U.S. Patent and Trademark Office and has represented clients in intellectual property cases before several district courts, the U.S. Court of Federal Claims, the International Trade Commission, the Federal Circuit, the Fourth Circuit, and the U.S. Supreme Court. Since entering private practice, he has successfully represented major pharmaceutical, electronics, and manufacturing companies in patent, copyright, trademark, and government contracts litigation. His practice also encompasses licensing and transactional work. While at the Department of Justice, he successfully represented more than fifty government agencies as lead trial and appellate counsel in numerous complex, multimillion-dollar patent lawsuits, as well as copyright and trademark cases. He has experience in both the liability and accounting phases of patent litigation, and he successfully defended the United States at both the trial and appellate levels against a $3 billion patent infringement claim involving satellite technology. He has also litigated cases involving classified technologies on behalf of the Central Intelligence Agency, the National Security Agency, and the Department of Defense in federal court proceedings.

Before entering the legal profession, Mr. Bergmann worked as an engineer for the Westinghouse Electric Corporation, designing nuclear power plants, and as a laboratory assistant at Princeton University. He has a degree in chemical engineering from Princeton University and attended law school at the University of Pittsburgh.

Contracts and Bidding on the State and Local Government Level: Key Considerations

Steven D. Weinstein

Partner

Blank Rome LLP

ASPATORE

In most cases, the government agency that issues a contract, or a request for a contract proposal, is the entity that administers, monitors, and enforces the contract. At a local government level, that could be a municipality, a county, or some specific agency, such as a county utilities authority. In addition, at the state level, within the state treasurer's office there is usually a division of purchase or property that may oversee a state government contract, depending on the subject matter and agency involved. Different states have different ways of applying general oversight, review, and enforcement to particular contracts. That responsibility may belong to an inspector general, for example, or a comptroller. However, contract oversight in the first instance would typically be handled by the particular agency that issues the contract.

Local government contracts may be issued by entities ranging from school boards to sewer authorities, and the contracts they issue could range from purchase contracts for paper or other supplies to contracts for professional services (e.g., engineering, legal services, or architectural services). Indeed, anything a government entity needs to buy, acquire, or obtain from sources outside of its own employees will require a contract. There is also a prescribed process by which an outside party can be awarded the contract—usually through some kind of bidding process—and there must also be a certification process to ensure that the government entity has the money to pay for the contract. Usually there is a statutory amount above which a public bidding process must take place. Below that statutory amount, there are instances in which the government purchasing personnel may award a contract directly without bidding, but a contract or purchase order will still be required.

Navigating Inter-Agency Contracting Efforts

The government contracting process is often a cooperative, inter-agency effort. If, for example, the state treasurer's office is responsible for the bidding of a contract, but the work being performed or the materials being acquired relate to a different agency in the state government, there has to be coordination between those agencies. Sometimes this process flows easily, but sometimes lawyers are needed to make sure the government and the contractor are on the same page, and that the necessary paperwork flows back and forth properly.

Many state and local agencies are now trying to work cooperatively on government contracts because there is a big push in many states to consolidate services to save money. For instance, various municipalities or local governments will often get together to buy insurance by pooling their risks (e.g., a county joint insurance fund that provides coverage for all the municipalities and school boards in the county), or several school districts will arrange cooperative contracts for busing services to create a larger-volume contract that will hopefully result in lower prices. Similarly, rather than having each school district arrange to buy school supplies on its own, a group of districts will often form a consortium to buy supplies in large volumes, to get lower pricing. Simply put, the goal of a cooperative contract is to lower the overall price for each agency, because the larger amount of goods or services creates greater leverage on pricing.

When a group of government agencies issues an inter-agency contract, there is an opportunity for private contractors to win larger-volume contracts. However, the nature of an inter-agency contract can also lead to problems, because when there is more than one government agency involved in a contract, the specifications that are issued are sometimes so general that they do not meet the specific aspects of what each governmental entity might want. That is probably not the case when a contract involves buying copy paper, but problems can arise when a contract involves more complicated items. For example, some school districts have considered bidding out and privatizing custodial services among different districts. However, every district is used to a certain level of service and certain times of the day when the service is provided. Therefore the school districts that are involved in the contract may not all be on the same page, and that may create complications for the company that is trying to bid on that contract. Therefore, an inter-agency contract has both good and bad aspects for private contractors.

Unique Aspects of Government Contract Law

There is a big difference between working with government agencies on contracts, as opposed to negotiating contracts in the private sector. In the private sector, one company can choose to negotiate with another company to come up with a contract the two sides agree upon, or one company can negotiate with many different companies to try to get the best contract price. This allows a great deal of flexibility when awarding a contract in the private sector.

However, when you are in a government contracting situation, there are laws that control how the contract goes out to bid, what has to be bid, and what does not have to be bid. If a contract must be offered for bidding, the government agency has to create written specifications for the service it is requesting, it has to publish those specifications, it has to provide a time period for people to respond, and it has to evaluate those responses to make sure they comply with all the requirements of the state's contracting statute. In most cases, the agency must award the contract to the lowest bidder. Conversely, in the private sector you may decide to award a contract to a higher-priced bidder because you like the quality of their work, you like working with that company, or they have a better reputation.

There are situations where a government agency may not have to award a contract to the lowest bidder through a process involving a request for proposals. Indeed, some statutes permit a government agency the option not to accept the lowest bid in certain very complicated contracting areas (e.g., operating and management of a waste water system or trash to steam plant). However, in the majority of cases in which a government agency puts out a contract specification, companies bid on the contract, and the agency has to take the lowest responsive and responsible bid. That sounds good in theory because the agency is getting the lowest price, but it reduces flexibility in the contracting process, and a bidder that can offer extra quality often loses out, because that extra quality might be priced a little higher than services offered by someone who bids lower, but does not offer the same quality of service.

Checklists for Government Contracts

When creating a checklist for clients who are involved in government contracting—whether you are representing the government or a private entity that wants to submit a bid or be awarded a contract—your first source of information should always be the statute that governs the bidding process. This is important because there are certain technical requirements that must be in the bid, the response, and the contract document that the successful bidder ultimately receives. Each state's government contracting statute will address the various certifications of bidders, the bid bond that might be required, and the terms of the contract that are permissible under that state statute. For example, a government contract must contain a description of the service or product the contract is meant to cover, and that product or service must be described with reasonable certainty so bidders will understand it and be on the same page. Sometimes the state statute will cover what the contract must contain, and sometimes it is left to the agency to determine what terms should be included.

In most cases, the more complicated the service, the more attention must be paid to how it is described in a government request for bid or contract. For example, let us say a state government is seeking to obtain marketing and operating services for a state lottery, which is a very complicated process. There is usually a statute or case law that requires certain elements to be contained in the contract terms for such a service, but there are other elements that would be unique in each case (e.g., the contract may involve certain highly technical requirements with respect to the purchase of the lottery machines, or it may involve less technical terms such as what kind of marketing and advertising services are needed, or what kind of oversight is expected). Similarly, a government contract for computer services may include specifications related to the capacity of computers the government is looking to buy, which may be based on general catalog descriptions, but if the government is looking to purchase software to run its accounts receivable or accounts payable systems, that software would have to be described in greater detail.

Consequently, practitioners in this area will typically utilize a combination of checklists, based on the state statute concerning government contracting, information provided by the agency that is offering the contract, and other checklists that most private entities/suppliers feel are appropriate. If you represent a private party submitting a bid, you must rely on those checklists to make sure all documentation is properly submitted with the bid, because the bid will be disqualified if you leave out certain information (e.g., if the bid requires the specific software requirements or outputs, a failure to include will result in rejection of the bid). Indeed, the biggest area of litigation with respect to government contracts involves someone who has been disqualified from the bidding process because they did not follow the checklist, or someone who believes the entity that won the bid did not follow the checklist.

Primary Goals when Working with the Government in Contract Law

The primary objective for a lawyer who is representing the government in a contract bidding process is to understand the statute pertaining to the contract, create a bidding document that meets the statutory and regulatory requirements and is specific enough to attract companies to want to submit a bid, and to be sure the bid is structured in such a way that you are getting the best price.

If you are representing a private entity that is bidding on a government contract, the perspective is a little different. First, you want to be sure your client understands the bid, and that a proposal is submitted that is responsive to that bid. If the bid is unclear in some way, it is important that you act early, because there is usually a period in which you can submit questions to get clarification on the terms of the bid. If you stay silent, submit a bid, and find out later that you lost out on the contract because you misunderstood it, you probably will not be able to challenge the contract award.

Unfortunately, many companies that submit bids on government contracts will do so on their own, and only consult a lawyer after a problem occurs—and in that instance, a lawyer's input may or may not have any effect on the situation. If the client misunderstood the terms of the written specification and, therefore, their bid is deemed non-responsive (i.e., they did not ask the proper questions because the bid was unclear), it may be too late to ask questions after the fact.

The Importance of Deadlines

It is critically important to keep in mind that when a bid specification is issued by a government agency, there is a time period in which to respond, and there is a time period before that during which you can ask questions if you need more clarity. Therefore, there is always some urgency involved in the bidding process to ensure you submit your questions and bids on time—simply put, you need to make sure your client fully understands the contract bid, and submits their response in a timely manner. Although the client is generally the one who determines the economics of what is being submitted in their response, it is the lawyer's job to ensure the bid is in proper form, because you will not often have the chance to correct any mistakes after submitting it.

In a deal involving two private companies, both parties will discuss the price that is being asked for, and the party that has submitted a price will have the freedom to change it later on, as will the company that wants to buy the service. However, in a government contracting situation, protections against fraud and favoritism are deemed vital, and everyone who is involved in the bidding process must be considered on an equal basis. After issuing a bid, the government does not have the right to say, "We will give a better explanation or more response time to Company A than we gave to Companies B or C." The government must give everyone the same explanations and timeframes. In addition, even though the government usually wants a service or product it is contracting for supplied fairly quickly, there is often a long timeframe in these deals, because the government first has to issue bids, accept bids, and then sign a contract. Therefore it is important to ensure you do not let any important deadlines slip by.

Making a Claim under Government Contracts

A client may sometimes wish to challenge a government contract that was awarded to another party, or another company may wish to challenge a contract that was awarded to your client. The chances of successfully challenging a government contract award will depend on whether the party that is making the challenge can provide any relevant legal factors for doing so. For example, if a client says, "My company is better than the company that won the bid," that would not be a sufficient reason to challenge a contract award, but you may be able to make a challenge if you believe the company that won the bid did not follow the rules.

If it is later in the process (e.g., your client has already won a contract) and the government is not paying the client or is threatening to revoke their contract because they think the client is not doing their job properly, the litigation process would be much the same as it would be in the private sector. In essence, your defense would be based on what the contract says and what the client did, or what the government says the client did not do properly.

Key Considerations in the Government Bidding Process

When you are looking to form a new working relationship with a government agency in the contract bidding context, the first thing you need to do is check the relevant statutes and regulations surrounding the bid. If a bid has already been issued, there may be restrictions as to who can talk to whom (e.g., whether the private company or its lawyer can communicate directly with the government during the bidding process). It is important to determine whether your client can start to develop a relationship with the government agency before the bidding is done, because if you fail to check the rules you could be thrown out of the bidding process. You may even face criminal charges if it is shown that you tried to influence the way the bid is structured or written. Consequently, you must fully understand the bidding environment, the agency that is offering the contract, the person who is awarding and reviewing the bid, and all of the statutes and regulations that control what the bidding process conversations can consist of.

In addition, you need to know how sophisticated and experienced your client is in terms of working with government agencies. A client that is used to working primarily in the private sector is used to having a lot more options and flexibility in how they approach the topic of a contract. Therefore, it is important to understand who your client is, whether they have done this kind of work before, and whether they have worked with this particular agency before.

Finally, you must assess if the contract in question involves a new subject area for the government agency that is issuing the contract. If the agency issues such a contract on a yearly basis, it has probably written a decent specification, but if the contract involves something the agency is doing for the first time, it may contain a lot of confusing elements—and in that case, you do not really know what you should be bidding, or what everybody else is bidding. Therefore, you need to determine whether you have the flexibility to ask questions early in the process, or if there is a formal period for submitting questions. It is always important to ask questions if there are terms you need to clarify, because once you have submitted your bid you cannot change it—and if you win the bid, you will be locked into the contract terms. You cannot say later on, "I won the bid because I was the low bidder, but I did not really understand the bid, and my price should have been a lot higher." Under government contract law statutes, you can usually revise a contract if you made an obvious mathematical mistake (e.g., pricing one hundred units at $10 a unit when the request for proposals called for 200 units), but if the mistake that was made is not so obvious, you will be stuck with the terms of your bid, even if it turns out that it is not the contract you thought you were bidding on.

Consequently, you really need to make sure your client and the government entity come to an understanding with respect to the contract terms within the timeframes that are permitted under the bidding process, so your client does not lose out on a contract they should have won—or win a contract and lose in the end, because they did not know what they were bidding on.

Compliance Issues When Working with Government Agencies

Compliance issues in the government contracting process will vary by state and locality, and there are compliance issues that are pertinent to the specifics of the bid as well. For example, a bid bond must be issued with a certain certification and signed off by an authorized person in your client's company, and it is important to know who the owners of the company are in order to ensure no one has been debarred or thrown off of contracts in the past.

There will also be a series of items that need to be reviewed in order to be sure you are compliant with the bid specification, including some very substantive compliance elements. For instance, in a janitorial program bid for a school or a government building, there may be requirements about the kinds of materials you must use (e.g., you must be sure they are "green" materials, or that they do not contain certain pesticides or other chemicals). If you are providing a service to clean asbestos out of a government building, you will need to comply with a whole range of environmental regulations about how you are going to perform that service. Essentially, the more technical the service that is being provided, the more important it is that you are compliant in all those regards.

Many compliance issues go beyond the subject of the bid, including those that pertain to political contributions. There are often numerous restrictions on how much a company or its partners or owners can spend in political contributions to the governing body (e.g., town or school district) that is issuing the contract. For example, if you are bidding on a government contract, you may not be able to make political contributions to the elected officials in your town for a certain period of time, and you have to certify that you have not done so. In addition, if you are awarded the contract you need to ensure you do not make any political contributions during the term of the contract. Sometimes those restrictions cover elected officials who are not directly related to the entity that issued the contract, including members of the state legislature. Each state has different regulations in this area, and you need to be sure of compliance in that regard as well.

Working Effectively with Government Agency Representatives

When working with government agency representatives in the contract bidding process, you need to remember that government employees have many job duties they must perform on a daily basis. Consequently, they have a focus that is pertinent to their particular job, and they do not necessarily understand the full scope of the services they are asking you to bid on. At the same time, they know they are being looked at through the prism of the public eye, and therefore they are generally very cautious in their approach to the government contract bidding process.

Therefore you need to understand the agency representative's level of expertise and sophistication in relation to the contract they are awarding, and be ready to work with them in a way that is best for your client. For example, if an agency employee says, "I want this type of contract because that is the type of contract I use with all private companies," you are not likely to have a lot of success if you start disputing the contract terms, because the government employee you are working with does not have the flexibility to change them. You have to follow certain parameters in the bidding process, always keeping in mind that the agency will generally use the same contract they used the last time they awarded that particular job, because someone in the government has already approved that contract.

Simply stated, if you want to move forward through the bidding process you have to understand who you are dealing with, what their goals are, and what rules they have to follow. In the private sector, two companies can agree to include virtually anything in a contract, as long as it is not illegal.

However, in the public sector a contract can only include things the statute says the government can do. You do not have the same flexibility you have in the private sector. First, there has to be a statute that says the government can issue a bid for a certain service or product, and that it can contract with someone privately. The statute will also say how the bidding has to be done—and you cannot go outside of the set of parameters the statute has set up. Obviously, you cannot do anything illegal in either setting, but flexibility is much greater in the private sector than it is in the government sector. Therefore, to successfully represent a private party in the government contract bidding process, you have to understand who you are dealing with in the public sector so the process can move along as expeditiously as possible.

Bidding Options

In the government contract bidding process, there are rules on what has to be bid and what does not, such as products or services that are below a certain financial threshold. You also have to know the bidding requirements (i.e., what has to be a strict bid, which usually translates into "the lowest price wins"). In some cases, instead of conducting a bidding process, the government will issue a request for proposal, which provides for some additional flexibility in the way you respond and the way you offer your services. In a request for proposal, there will still be criteria against which a proposal will be judged, but the notice of the service may be more open-ended. For example, most professionals now contract through requests for proposals, which allow a broader description of experience and services to be provided. Alternatively, the agency may ask you to respond to a request for qualification, which is like a pre-proposal. In other words, the government is allowed to qualify who is going to submit bids. This most frequently occurs with highly technical proposals. For example, awarding the operation of an energy plant will start with qualifying who can bid to avoid a low bid by a company with no experience in that area.

The more sophisticated the service the government is contracting for, the more complexity is likely to be involved in the bidding process. These are the circumstances where first qualifying as a bidder is likely. This is a totally different process than a "pure bid," where you submit the necessary papers and the price you are bidding, and someone at the government agency picks a winner. Each state has different regulations, and even the federal government does not have uniform rules in this area, because it has so many different agencies.

It can be very difficult to understand the bidding rules in all fifty states if you are a national provider, as opposed to a company that serves agencies in just one state. For example, if you are a company that provides cafeteria food services to school districts all over the country, you need to understand what the bidding rules are in each state. Or if you are an engineering firm that provides services to governments across the country in terms of managing their buildings, energy systems, or construction projects, you need to be aware that each state has its own set of bidding rules. The rules in each location may fill many books, but you need to become familiar with those rules if you do not want to run afoul of the laws in one state, simply because you followed the rules that were in effect in another state.

Contract Law Violations and Agency Audits

You are most likely to face an agency audit for contract violations if you are found to have repeated failures to satisfy the requirements in one contract category—and depending on what the contract covers, avoiding such violations can be simple or more complex. Over-billing will definitely result in an audit, and if you do not submit billing documents in the proper fashion, you may also face an audit, because you may be suspected of violations involving fraud, kickbacks, and bribes.

For example, if you do not submit your bills promptly and you suddenly submit one bill for six months of work without properly certifying your expenses, you are likely to face a financial audit. There are also performance audits in terms of the quality of the work you perform, which do not happen nearly as frequently as financial audits, but may be more likely to occur, depending on the nature of the service.

Efficiency in the Bidding Process

The government contracting process is aimed at avoiding fraud and favoritism. Its goal is to be open, and to put all bidders on an equal footing, so the government agency representative who is handing out the contract cannot simply give it to a friend or other inside people, and so more criminal activities are avoided. The regulations surrounding the government contract process stem from the fact that the government is paying the contractor with taxpayer money, and therefore its bidding process needs to be clean, proper, and above board. All bidders need to be on an equal footing so the government gets the best price or the best service for the contract it is awarding.

However, the government's bidding process is not necessarily the most efficient way of operating a bidding process, because there are so many technical steps that need to be followed. For example, if I own a private company and I have already used another company fifteen times to provide various services, I can simply pick up the phone and tell that company I need another service, and I will then ask them whether they can do the job, and what their price would be. That is a much more efficient way of obtaining products and services than a bidding process, and I may not even need a written contract, depending on what the service is.

There is also a misconception that a competitive bidding process always gets you the lowest price and the best service, and neither of those beliefs is necessarily correct. May companies avoid even submitting bids because they don't want to deal with all the rules.

Consequently, there is always a challenge involved in increasing the efficiency of a bidding process in a government setting, and indeed, one of the jobs of a government contract lawyer is to try to move that process along as efficiently as possible. To that end, you need to scour the bid documents to make sure your client's bid is technically correct, and ask the right questions. Once you submit the bid, you need to follow up to see who the bid is ultimately awarded to, to determine if you can file a challenge. Follow-up is also needed if your client wins the award. A bidding process involving a local government agency is generally run by the purchasing agent, but the award of the contract often requires the town council's approval. Therefore you need to make sure this process takes place, and then you need to make sure your client receives a written contract—at which point, the lawyer is no longer involved in the contract process, unless problems occur.

Efficiency is always a big issue in the government contracting process, because the government usually does not operate in an urgent manner, and there are so many procedures you need to go through.

Final Thoughts: Working with Clients in Government Contracting

Clients who have done a lot of business with government agencies in many jurisdictions will typically have much more experience in this area than someone who is involved in the bidding process for the first time—or someone who is moving from one jurisdiction to another, and thinks they know what they are doing because they did things a certain way in Pennsylvania, only to find out there is a whole different process in New Jersey.

In addition, things may change over the course of a contract, and you may or may not be able to change the pricing accordingly. For instance, if you are supplying food to a government agency, there is usually some provision you can include in the contract (e.g., a mark-up contract provision) that allows you to adjust the price over time, because price is subject to so many external factors. However, if a client is not familiar with all of these rules, they may get stuck with a contract where they bid a certain price for a three-year period. This can be very problematic in the current economy. Who could have predicted three years ago how much the price of oil would affect the price of transportation, which in turn affected food prices? It is important to make provisions for such instances in a government contract.

Finally, it is important for clients and their lawyers to keep in mind that the rules in this area vary by each government jurisdiction, and there are big differences between contracting in the public and private sectors. Simply put, in the private sector two companies can get together and decide what they want to do in a business arrangement, as long as it is legal. But in the public sector, you cannot do that, and that really controls everything else that goes on in the bidding process.

Steven D. Weinstein is a partner with Blank Rome LLP. His practice concentrates on contract, commercial, environmental, and trademark litigation; administrative law; governmental relations; local and state government law; local and state redevelopment and incentives; and higher education law. He also works on cases involving public finance practice, representing numerous local government units, authorities, and underwriters in municipal bond transactions and related matters, and in administrative matters, litigation, and government relations.

Mr. Weinstein is a certified New Jersey state and federal mediator. He is admitted to practice before the U.S. Court of Claims, the U.S. Third Circuit Court of Appeals, the U.S. Supreme Court, the U.S. District Court of New Jersey, the U.S. District Court for the Eastern District of Pennsylvania, and in both Pennsylvania and New Jersey. He is a member of the New Jersey State Bar Association, the Camden County Bar Association, the American Bar Association, the Association of Trial Lawyers of America, and other professional organizations. He has also held numerous governmental positions. He earned his B.A. from Rutgers College and his J.D. from the Rutgers-Camden School of Law. He has been listed in Who's Who in the East, Who's Who in American Law, Who's Who—Emerging Leaders in America, *and* Men of Achievement.

New Strategies and Challenges for Government Contractors

Matthew Koehl

Partner

K&L Gates LLP

ASPATORE

The Department of Defense and certain civilian agencies, including the General Services Administration (GSA), the Department of Health and Human Services, and the Department of Veterans Affairs, award and administer the most federal government contracts. However, all other executive agencies have a significant role in the award, administration, and enforcement of federal government contracts.

The GSA manages the largest contract program for "commercial item" products and services, the GSA multiple award schedule (MAS) contract program. Annual reported MAS contract sales were approximately $36 billion in the most recent government fiscal year. Note that the term "commercial item" is defined in Federal Acquisition Regulation (FAR) 48 CFR § 2.101. The scope of the commercial item definition is extremely broad and reasonably includes virtually any product or service similar to those available in the commercial marketplace. All executive agencies are eligible to place task and delivery orders against GSA MAS contracts.

The Department of Defense awards more non-commercial item contracts, including contracts for weapons and weapons systems and research and development. These types of Department of Defense contracts tend more frequently to be awarded as cost reimbursement contracts. Broadly speaking, a cost reimbursement contractor will receive payment for its costs of contract performance (including overhead, and general and administrative costs) plus a reasonable profit, with the government bearing the risk of cost overruns compared to the estimated cost at the time of award. See, e.g., FAR Subpart 16.3, Cost-Reimbursement Contracts. This contrasts with the preferred structure of fixed price contracts, where the contractor agrees to perform a specific requirement for a fixed price and bears the risk of cost overruns (but keeps the additional profit where performance costs are less than anticipated). See, e.g., FAR Subpart 16.2, Fixed Price Contracts.

The Role of State and Local Governments in Contract Law

All states have laws and implementing regulations (as well as unpublished guidance) that specify the rules that must be followed when awarding and administering public contracts. Contracting rules at the state and local government level tend to be less comprehensive and are often less formal than the federal procurement law system. The rules for state and local government contracting often mirror the federal procurement system, but will invariably differ in some respects. For example, the protected categories for the standard equal employment opportunity contract clause, as well as small and minority business contracting categories and requirements, vary by state and local jurisdiction.

Litigation involving state and local government contracts must generally be resolved in the applicable state or local courts or administrative dispute resolution tribunals. This is the case both with bid protests challenging contract formation and litigation relating to contract administration and performance issues.

As at the federal level, the laws relating to government contracting are passed by the applicable legislative body, with implementation of such laws being the responsibility of the executive branch agencies.

Like the federal government, every state has some type of agency that is charged with health and welfare, as well as an agency charged with purchasing many or most items on behalf of the state government (e.g., general services administration, department of general services, state purchasing division). These state agencies are often less formal, although not necessarily more flexible, as compared to their federal agency counterparts. At the same time, state agencies can be less knowledgeable about basic procurement law rules and requirements than their federal counterparts are. State and local agencies can also be more parochial and more subject to influence by factors not based in contract law, including political considerations.

State and local government agencies are sometimes authorized to purchase from federal purchasing vehicles (i.e., "cooperative purchasing" under the GSA MAS Schedule 70 program for information technology hardware, software, and professional services). State and local government contracts funded in whole or in part with federal government-provided funding are often subject to certain federal government contract requirements.

Cooperative Arrangements in Government Contract Awards Programs

Government agencies often purchase through contracts awarded by other agencies. This can affect the specific contract requirements applicable to government agency contracts. For example, the GSA—and the Department of Veterans Affairs, for medical products—awards long-term MAS contracts. MAS contracts are open for orders from all other executive agencies (and other entities), but are governed by the GSA (or Department of Veterans Affairs) negotiated terms and conditions except to the extent additional terms or conditions are included in a particular agency task or delivery order placed against the contract. Many other agencies have awarded government-wide acquisition contracts that are open to all other government agencies. The GSA administers contracts on behalf of other agencies, the Department of Defense in particular, where the "end user" agency lacks adequate procurement staff. There are other inter-agency contracts and transfers of excess property.

At the same time, each agency has agency-specific regulatory supplements to the FAR with deviations and additional regulatory requirements. It is important to understand these agency-unique differences. For instance, the Air Force FAR Supplement incorporates additional guidance with regard to ethics rules and standards for Air Force personnel. Air Force FAR Supplement Part 5303, "Improper Business Practices and Personal Conflicts of Interest."

Challenges in Government Contract Law

When working in the area of government contract law, it is important to understand current policy initiatives and considerations that can affect implementation and interpretation of regulations and requirements. For example, the Department of Defense has recently been concerned about pricing on "commercial item" contracts, and has sometimes been less flexible in allowing contractors to avoid providing certified cost or pricing data even where the applicable FAR rules would seem to exempt the procurement from this requirement.

The challenges of working on cost reimbursement and commercial item contracts tend to be fairly consistent across agencies. However, GSA MAS contracts are far more complex and risky than other types of federal commercial item contracting. This is due to the "defective pricing" and "price reductions" provisions in GSA MAS contracts, which are non-commercial, burdensome, and create substantial opportunity for fines and penalties. This risk is exacerbated by the GSA Office of Inspector General's aggressive audit posture in recent years. There are also some unique challenges when working with the Department of Homeland Security on government contracts. The Department of Homeland Security began operations in March 2003 and, according to the Government Accountability Office, has not developed the necessary acquisition workforce to meet its contracting requirements. A November 2008 Government Accountability Office report confirmed previous findings that the Department of Homeland Security did not have adequate staff to plan and execute contracts for complex Department of Homeland Security requirements. See www.gao.gov/new.items/d0930.pdf. Such a contracting environment can be fertile ground for schedule delays and contract claims and disputes.

Checklists of Key Issues

The checklist of key issues when working with agencies on public health contracts would necessarily be driven by the requirements in the applicable solicitation or request for proposal. In general, the checklist would be the standard checklist for FAR Part 12 commercial item contracting plus, possibly, (i) Privacy Act, (ii) human health and safety issues, (iii) animal welfare issues, and (iv) record maintenance issues.

In other cases, the checklist of key issues in a government contract will be driven by the solicitation requirements. There are certain types of contracts that will have unique and often complex issues, including (i) cost accounting issues on cost reimbursement contracts, (ii) intellectual property issues on research and development contracts, (iii) defective pricing practices disclosures and price reductions issues on GSA MAS contracts, (iv) Trade Agreements Act compliance issues on large supply contracts, and (v) small business size status issues on small business set-aside contracts. For example, where the small business is contemplating a merger or acquisition with another business at the time it bids on a set-aside contract, this can result in loss of small business status even where the transaction is not complete.

Recent Trends in Government Contract Law

Changes in government contract law tend to be cyclical. For instance, in the 1990s the emphasis was on procurement reform to allow greater agency buyer discretion and to encourage commercial companies to enter the government market by removing government contract-unique barriers to entry. More recently, the pendulum has swung towards greater government oversight and contractor ethics accountability and strict compliance with contract requirements (i.e., the recent contractor ethics rule mandating disclosure of possible violations of law, and requiring contractor codes of business conduct and internal compliance and control systems).

Changes in government contract law are generally foreshadowed in industry publications and commentary, draft rules, and congressional hearings. Change tends to be less frequent and comprehensive on the state and local level versus the federal level, perhaps in part due to the few government resources available to focus full-time on public procurement issues. Specific events in a state or local jurisdiction can also result in change. (For example, the sole-source contract awarded in 2001 by the state of California to Oracle under questionable circumstances, which resulted in a comprehensive review and publication of recommendations to overhaul of California state contracting rules for information technology. The specifics involved in the award of a sole-source $95 million contract to Oracle that allegedly would have cost the state $41 million more than existing contracts. The contract was later canceled, and California's governor returned a $25,000 contribution from Oracle, the propriety of which had been questioned. See news.cnet.com/2100-1017_3-994273.html.)

Of all the recent changes in government contract law, the new contractor ethics and disclosure rule implemented through FAR 52.203-13 has had the greatest impact on my practice. This rule creates a substantial new contractor obligation to disclose possible violations of certain laws (fraud, conflicts of interest, bribery, and false claims), but provides very little guidance as to how these new standards are to be applied.

Primary Goals when Working with Government Agencies

At a micro-level, the primary goal when working with government agencies in the area of government contract law is to help the government agency understand how to purchase products and services as efficiently as possible, with as few government-unique requirements as possible, while still including all requirements applicable to the type and size of the contract being awarded. There has been a significant reduction in the number and quality of government procurement professionals over the past fifteen years, which has made this task more difficult—and more necessary.

At a macro-level, the goal is helping government agencies identify procurement reform initiatives that will simplify the contracting process—thereby allowing government procurement to be "better, faster, cheaper"—while still ensuring that the government's interests are protected. For instance, some executive agencies have been able to award blanket purchase agreements under the MAS program for large, recurring commodity item requirements in a fraction of the time and with substantially less administrative burden and bid protest risk and delay than a standard "full and open" competition procurement. The pricing obtained for these blanket purchase agreements is often highly competitive, notwithstanding the streamlined evaluation and award process. Programs like this that have worked should be continued.

The narrow objectives are typically identified and developed in consultation with the client to quantify the burdens and risks presented by a particular government procurement, and to identify possible ways to reduce or eliminate unnecessary burdens and risks. At the macro-level, these objectives are often identified by industry trade groups and professional associations, such as the Technology Association of America, the National Contract Management Association, the Coalition for Government Procurement, the American Bar Association public contract law section, the Council of Defense and Space Industries, and so on.

Factors that often affect the urgency of working with government agencies include the size and significance of the contract at issue, including strategic considerations for follow-on contract work, intellectual property development, and so on, and the magnitude of the government contract's unique risks and burdens that may be subject to reduction or elimination through the structuring of the contract.

Challenges often ensue in the contractor/government agency relationship due to different priorities for government (i.e., avoiding risk) than industry, and lack of resources on either side to handle contract issues.

Forming a Working Relationship with a Government Agency

There are typically two key steps in forming a new working relationship with a government agency in the area of contracts law:

1. Make sure to understand the general and agency-unique rules (if any) that are applicable to your particular contracts.
2. Make sure to understand the relationship between the agency procurement shop and program personnel as relevant to your contracts.

Step 1 is driven by the underlying government requirements and procurement documents and planning. The client plays a key role in this step by helping to identify specific requirements and a complete list of procurement documents.

Step 2 is driven by the specifics of each procurement situation. The client's input is critical to understanding the relationship of the agency's program personnel to the procurement personnel and, in particular, understanding any ability the program personnel may have to influence timeliness and flexibility by the agency's procurement group. For instance, will it be possible to tailor the terms and conditions of a commercial item contract (FAR 52.212-4) to match the contractor's standard commercial terms for inspection/acceptance, thereby allowing the contractor to avoid deferring recognition of all or some of the contract revenue and making the contract more financially desirable?

Several strategies are often successfully used to pursue client goals when working with government agencies in the contracting area:

- Play dumb (i.e., "The regulations seem to say this is not a requirement for this type of contract. Am I missing the point?").
- Have your client's advocates in the program office encourage the contracting office personnel to be flexible in negotiating contract terms. For instance, where the contractor fears an industry shortage and/or price increase for a certain item (e.g., steel), modify the contract to (i) specifically identify industry-wide supply shortages as an "excusable delay" event, and (ii) provide for automatic economic price adjustment for increased prices based upon a published third-party pricing index.

Government Contractor Checklists

When prepping contractor clients to work with government agencies, I always use a "checklist for compliance" document for commercial item contractors, which identifies all government-unique requirements that could generally apply to contractors performing contracts for commercial items. I use an amended checklist for compliance for commercial item contractors performing GSA MAS contracts. Contractors performing research and development work, other cost reimbursement work, and classified contracts would have other items on a standard checklist.

The client checklist must account for agency-unique requirements. These range from the significant to the non-material or inapplicable (e.g., a "specialty metals" clause included in a Department of Defense contract for computer software). The additional agency-unique requirements are generally specified in the agency request for proposal. Certain types of contracts contain unique additional requirements in addition to the list of basic considerations applicable to commercial item prime contracts. These include, in particular:

- MAS contract pricing issues, including the requirement to submit "current, accurate, and complete" pre-award commercial sales practices disclosures and post-award pricing obligations under the MAS contract price reductions clause
- Intellectual property ownership under cost reimbursement and research and development contracts, including marking of technical

data and making required notifications and disclosures to the government

- Cost accounting considerations under cost reimbursement contracts, including the cost principles in FAR Part 31 and the requirements of the Cost Accounting Standards (applicable to large government contractors)
- Trade Agreements Act compliance under large supply contracts, which require the contractor to supply only "end products" from the United States and other specified "designated countries" for the entire term of the contract
- Classified contracting issues, including the requirements of the National Security Program Industrial Operations Manual, Department of Defense 5220.22-M
- Small business set-aside contracting issues, including knowledge of the Small Business Administration's detailed rules and interpretative case law defining when two firms are "affiliates" and therefore treated as a single entity for size determination purposes

Compliance Issues

Government contracts contain unique requirements and must be taken seriously. The specific requirements for compliance efforts will be dictated by the size and type of government contracts the client holds. These can range from a few modest equal employment opportunity-type requirements for a commercial item subcontractor (much less is generally required on commercial item contracts) to a compliance program for cost reimbursement contractors that will cost millions of dollars to establish and maintain. Therefore, all procedures and policies must be tailored based upon specific contract requirements. In general, training, internal audits, and knowledgeable staff are key to successful compliance efforts.

The contractor must understand each government contract-unique requirement that applies to it by virtue of its specific government prime contracts and subcontracts. It must then develop policies and procedures—appropriate for the size of the company and the types of government contracts it holds and the associated requirements—to reasonably assure compliance.

There is no "one size fits all" approach to compliance in this area, but in general, a government contract law compliance program should include a tailored code of business ethics and conduct; regular compliance training for company employees who have a role in ensuring compliance with each of the company's specific government contract requirements (e.g., sales and bid desk for MAS contract price reductions compliance, or human resources for equal employment opportunity and affirmative action requirements); regular internal compliance audits where the company's internal audit and/or third-party experts conduct a detailed, independent review of compliance with specific company government contract requirements (e.g., a review of whether the company has an effective system to ensure it complies with the requirement to supply only domestic end products under a supply contract covered by the Buy American Act, or that the company is paying its workers required wages and benefits and preserving payroll records under a construction contract subject to the Davis Bacon Act); a compliance hotline; and a trained compliance officer holding a senior position within the company.

With respect to compliance investigations and enforcement proceedings, each case is unique. General principles include:

- Thoroughly and quickly investigate relevant facts.
- Take steps to preserve privilege whenever possible.
- Cooperate with government auditors and investigators, but do not roll over unnecessarily.
- Establish a single point of contact for government auditors and investigators.
- Keep management well informed.
- Take remedial action as necessary. For instance, if a company discovered it had not been accurately charging employee time under its government contracts, it would need to promptly revise its time charging procedures and train applicable to employees to ensure that time charged to government contracts is accurate and in compliance with all contract requirements.
- Keep thorough documentation of all facets of the company's investigation of the issue, in consultation with counsel and giving

due regard to maintaining the privilege that might be applicable to certain documents.

- Disclose where necessary, keeping in mind the recent FAR rule implemented via FAR Clause 52.203-13, which rule, where applicable, requires contractors to disclose to the government suspected violations of certain laws (fraud, conflicts of interest, bribery, and false claims).

Performance Issues in Contract Law

To avoid disputes in the performance of a government contract, it is important for both parties to fully understand the underlying contractual requirements that could affect the parties' respective rights relating to the performance issues. It is important to keep in mind that the government agency is the customer—and to be friendly, but firm.

Strategy is always developed in conjunction with the client, understanding and considering their long-term goals and objectives. Performance issues that are the most critical, from a contract law perspective, include timely delivery/completion of projects, documented compliance with contract requirements, and ethical conduct.

Client Responsibilities when Working with Government Agencies

Government officials have substantial discretion when making procurement law decisions, and this can work for or against the contractor, depending on its relationship with the contracting officer. Simply put, good relations and a commitment to government customer satisfaction can result in more flexibility and better contractual relations with the government. Happy customers tend to be much more flexible, which is especially helpful given the high degree of discretion agency personnel often have with regard to procurement law decisions.

Client responsibilities when working with government agencies in the contracting area include establishing exclusive contact with agency program personnel to ensure the client is meeting performance requirements, and establishing principal contact with the agency contracting officer.

It is important for an attorney in this practice area to prepare several contingencies or fail-safes in the event that clients are not able to fully contribute to the contractor-agency relationship (i.e., provide options to "off-load" responsibilities where the client lacks resources or expertise to fulfill its responsibilities). For instance, recommend that the contractor hire a knowledgeable government contract professional to administer its government contracts, or an accountant specializing in government contracts to review its incurred cost submissions to the government. It might also be advisable in certain circumstances to recommend that the client make the agency aware of its limitations. For instance, a MAS contract reseller that is unable to determine the extent of rebates it will receive from subcontractor/manufacturer partners until the end of a quarter or year—and therefore is unable to effectively pass on the benefit of possible rebates to individual MAS contract orders—should disclose this to the GSA and expressly disavow a duty to monitor the effect of such rebates on its MAS contract pricing.

Difficulties in Completing a Government Contract

Various factors contribute to difficulties in obtaining and completing a government contract, including a poorly drafted and ambiguous request for proposal and contract terms, which can lead to both bid protests and contract performance and administration disputes. Other factors affecting performance may include inadequate agency resources and expertise, inefficient or conflicting administration by government personnel, and unreasonable individuals on either or both sides.

It is difficult to generalize with respect to which agencies resolve issues most quickly. The Air Force sometimes seems better at handling these issues than the Navy or Army. The GSA and the Department of Veterans Affairs are sometimes more difficult than other civilian agencies, in part, according to some, because of their respective Office of Inspector General. Fortunately, most agencies have done a very good job of making resources available online for contractors and their counsel, including both the GSA and the Department of Defense.

Assisting Clients with Government Agency Interactions

Clients often have a broad range of experience in terms of dealing with government agencies in the area of contract law. Some commercial companies with just a few public-sector clients have very limited agency interaction in contract law. The contract terms for such clients are often commercial and the dollar value low, so problems are often avoided, but this situation can result in serious compliance problems. However, full-time government contractors often have daily interaction with all government agencies, and have the in-house expertise to handle these issues properly.

Significant internal resources and expertise in this area can reduce the client's need for our services and for general hand-holding. At the same time, smaller and inexperienced clients are sometimes able to be held to a lower standard by government contracting officers and auditors, in recognition of their lesser sophistication with often complex government contract requirements and fewer resources available for formal, detailed contracting policies and procedures.

Executives or managers who are generally the best prepared for involvement with contracting agencies include bid or proposal and contract management, and government sales executives. Naturally, full-time government contractors are uniquely experienced in agency activities. Conversely, the nature of their business and the unique requirements for non-commercial item contractors require the creation of infrastructure, training, and expertise in government-unique requirements.

Managing Documents

Comprehensive checklists must generally be compiled to manage documents in each client's government contracting case. However, each case is unique. Therefore, you should prepare checklists based upon prior examples, updated to account for the unique considerations of the current case.

Usually an associate or client contract manager or in-house attorney prepares the contract-related documents, at the direction of experienced outside counsel. Cost-reimbursement and research and development contracts tend to generate significant amounts of documents relating to incurred costs and technical and scientific data.

Questions When Handling a Claim against a Government Contract

Despite efforts on both sides of a contracting relationship, government agencies frequently become the subject of a claim on the part of a government contractor. Key questions that should be asked when handling a claim for a contractor client against a government agency include:

- What is the factual predicate for the claim?
- What documents/facts are necessary to prove legal entitlement to recover on the claims asserted against the agency?
- Assuming the contractor can demonstrate entitlement to recover some amount, what documents/facts are necessary to prove claim quantum (i.e., the amount of the recovery)?
- What notice of the claim was provided to the government contracting officer?
- Are any other parties involved in the claim facts (e.g., subcontractors)?
- Which sections of the contract and contract requirements are at issue?
- Have there been negotiations on the claim?
- Was a request for equitable adjustment filed?
- Can you confirm there are no modifications waiving the claim?

Understanding the factual and legal bases of the claim, as well as how difficult the claim may be to support and possible defenses to the claim, impacts the degree of effort that should be devoted to the claim (or even whether the claim should be pursued at all).

Dispute resolution alternatives range from informal discussions to letter writing to formal adjudication of disputes in administrative tribunals or federal court. Less formality is generally best for the client, in significant part because it keeps costs low and can result in a less adversarial posture with the agency customer. However, the nature of the dispute and the specific agency personnel involved can drive different methods for working with agency personnel on contract law issues. For example, where agency contracting personnel appear to be unwilling to compromise or otherwise engage reasonably to resolve a contract dispute, the contractor may be well advised to select a more formal dispute resolution process with an independent party (e.g., administrative law judge) capable of resolving issues disputed by the parties. The Armed Services Board of Contract Appeals and the Civilian Board of Contract Appeals are available for formal resolution of contractor claims. The Court of Federal Claims also decides claims litigation involving government contracts and, in general, has more procedural formality.

Contract Law Violations and Outcomes

Government contract law violations or perceived violations that are the most likely to result in an agency audit include those involving GSA MAS contract pricing issues; employee qualifications; Trade Agreement Act compliance (i.e., the requirement to supply only "end products" from the United States or certain other "designated countries"); gifts and gratuities, kickbacks, and other ethical issues; and improper time charging. Audits are often the result of government auditor perception of contractor non-compliance risk areas, or recent past documented violations and whistleblower reports.

There is a broad range of possible outcomes in an agency audit, depending on the seriousness, size, and length of the problem, and whether the contractor brought the issue to the government's attention or responded properly to evidence of a possible violation. Outcomes range from no material negative consequences, to any of the following (sometimes in concert): (i) fines and penalties, in particular, under the civil False Claims Act, (ii) contract termination for default or cancellation, and (iii) suspension or debarment proceedings.

Protesting a Government Contract Bid

Protesting a government contract bid is always problematic, because you are, in effect, suing your customer. Further, you often win the protest but do not win the contract, and in the meantime, you have made an enemy of agency contracting and/or program personnel. The outcomes range from losing your protest, to winning the protest but not winning the contract (either because the agency cancels the procurement or selects a competitor the second time around), to winning the contract. It is very rare for the Government Accountability Office or the courts to direct an award to the protesting contractor. It is generally left up to the agency, even if the protest succeeds.

Procedural unfairness tends to be the most successful protest grounds. Pre-award challenges to request for proposal terms and competitive range exclusions tend to be more effective than protests attempting to dislodge an awarded contract.

Key considerations before initiating a protest include:

- Did the agency follow the terms of the request for proposal?
- Can you establish prejudice from agency errors?
- Is my protest timely under the strict rules for agency level and Government Accountability Office bid protest submissions?
- What are the long-term consequences to customer relations from protesting?
- What is the best forum based upon specific facts of this protest, including timeliness considerations and the long-term relationship with the agency (agency, Government Accountability Office, or Court of Federal Claims)? This should be a comprehensive determination with input from sales/business development and protest counsel.

Final Thoughts

In conclusion, I would advise all lawyers and clients working with government agencies in the area of government contract law to always do the following:

- Focus very closely on the requirements included in your specific contracts.
- Take advantage of information available on government Web sites.

- Read cases involving your specific issues and questions. Quite often, the issue you face has been faced and decided before.
- Always read the applicable regulations closely. They often answer even complex or obscure questions.

Matthew Koehl is a partner with K&L Gates LLP. His practice has focused for more than fifteen years on representing companies that transact business with federal, state, and local government agencies, with a special emphasis on the federal General Services Administration multiple award schedule program. He has extensive bid protest experience involving contracts awarded by federal, state, and local government agencies, having represented contractors in more than forty bid protest proceedings before the courts and administrative tribunals. He has worked on numerous merger and acquisition projects involving government contractors, representing both buyers and sellers. In addition, he has helped companies create and implement compliance programs and conduct internal audits and investigations.

Prior to joining K&L Gates, Mr. Koehl spent five years as the general counsel to MicronPC Government, a leading General Services Administration Schedule 70 contractor, and a top-three PC supplier to the federal government.

Appendices

Appendix A: Recent Developments and Issues in Government Investigations 92

Appendix B: Compliance Plan Table of Contents 109

Appendix C: Conducting Business in the Federal Government Marketplace 112

Appendix D: Federal Acquisition Regulation, Part 27 125

Appendix E: Federal Acquisition Regulation, Part 52 184

APPENDIX A

RECENT DEVELOPMENTS AND ISSUES IN GOVERNMENT INVESTIGATIONS

Current Government Contracts Work Snapshot

Government Investigation-Related Work

- Grand Jury subpoenas
- Inspector General subpoenas
    - Tend to see these for large high-profile projects gone bad
    - Typical Issues include:
        - Fraud (time charging/billing issues)
        - Ethics/conflicts/hiring issues
- DoL SCA/DBA counseling and investigations
- Responses to suspension/debarment show cause orders

Government Contracts Compliance Work

- Conduct on-site audits (proactive and reactive)
    - Review/revise policies and procedures
    - Remediation work
- Develop/implement compliance programs
- Increased activity/interest in this area with:
    - New proposed FAR rules that would mandate compliance programs for most non-commercial item contractors

  - New legislation targeted at responsibility determinations of DoD Contracting Officers where a contractor does not have an internal compliance program

<u>General Counseling and Protest Work</u>

- Commercial item "push back"

  - DoD primes and others are feeling the pressure

  - Reaction to recent DoD IG Report critical of commercial item contracting practices

  - Recent DFARS Final Rule and Air Force guidance significantly limiting acquisition of major weapons systems as commercial items

  - The 2008 DAA (S 1547) also contains provisions (sections 822 & 823) that seek to further curtail use of commercial item/services under certain circumstances

  - Proposed FAR Case 2007-006 would extend mandatory code of ethics and disclosure requirements to large commercial item contractors

- Increased use of rated orders and potential criminal penalties for non-compliance

- High-profile protest work

Recent Developments and Issues in Government Investigations

- National Procurement Fraud Task Force

- DoJ Alliances Investigation

- FCA Qui Tam Litigation Developments

- Suspension and Debarment Proceedings

- Other Legislative Developments
- OCIs and PIA
- Iraq Contracting Audit

National Procurement Fraud Task Force (NPFTF)

- Announced in connection with $98M Oracle settlement for GSA defective pricing in October 2006
- NPFTF published a July 2007 "white paper" report
- Report proposes strengthening the tools available to the Federal Government to "detect, prevent and prosecute procurement and grant fraud."
- Currently twenty-nine regional coordinators/offices

July 2007 Task Force Report

- First area of concentration: Improve internal codes of ethics of grantees and contractors
  - Proposes legislation to require development of internal code of ethics and reporting requirements for government contractors that goes beyond proposed FAR rule
- Second area of concentration: Improve Government ability to prevent and detect procurement fraud
  - Proposes legislation requiring timely reports from grantees and contractors of Government overpayment
  - Proposes expansion of criminal conflict of interests provisions of 18 U.S.C. §208
  - Proposes reinstating audit rights for GSA OIG over pricing information in GSA MAS contracts

- Proposes establishment of national procurement fraud database

- Many components of each of these recommendations were included in proposed FAR Rules (FAR Cases 2006-07 and 2007-06)

- <u>Third area of concentration</u>: Improve prosecution and adjudication of fraud

  - Amend sentencing guidelines to broadly define "economic loss"

  - Draft legislation created that allows OIG to compel interviews under subpoena authority

  - Increase cooperation between OIG attorneys and DOJ

- <u>Other ideas for changes:</u>

  - Improve audit access rights

    - NRO Model using contractual language

  - Recommends changes to Procurement Integrity Act, 41 U.S.C. §423

    - Re-examine/expand remedies provision to increase use of this statute

  - False Claims Act, 31 U.S.C. §3731(b)

    - Extend FCA statute of limitations for criminal and civil cases to 10 and 15 years, respectively

  - Incentivize agencies to actively pursue fraud

    - Credit back recoveries to agency coffers as opposed to a general Treasury fund?

- Establish a working capital fund for certain fraud investigatory efforts?

DOJ Alliances Investigation

- Broad industry-wide subpoena targeting technology vendors and systems integrators or other "third party objective advisers" to the Government

- Primarily focusing on "channel distribution model" of selling to the Government:

  - Technology vendors providing alliance benefits to systems integrators who advise and sell to the government in the form of rebates, referral fees, and marketing development funds

  - Government says that these business practices were not fully disclosed, resulting in:

    - False claims for payment submitted to the Government (*i.e.*, artificially inflated prices);

    - Organizational conflicts of interest; and

    - Defective GSA schedule pricing (*i.e.*, failing to reflect rebates/discounts/etc.)

- DOJ is actively pursuing litigation through filing of complaints against HP, Sun and Accenture

- Other companies are also subject to ongoing investigation, but no formal intervention or declination for many as of yet

- Settlements reached with some companies (IBM, CSC and PwC have settled with the Government)

- Has forced other companies to take a hard look at their practices in this area to see if they fall within scope of Government's allegations

- Difficult to make broad generalizations as a result of this experience at this point because investigation/litigation is still ongoing and because many of the business practices under investigation were/are standard industry practices

- We have crafted a "Do's and Don'ts" memo to assist clients that identifies strategies for reducing risk in this area

Qui Tam Litigation Developments

- Many cases decided in 2006 and early 2007 impact *qui tam* litigation in areas such as presentment, original source/public disclosure bar, statute of limitations, release and mistake versus false claim

- Some of these decisions appear to support a more narrow reading of the scope of the *qui tam* provisions, contrary to a movement that had been broadening its application

- Presentment and Intent – *Allison Engine Co. v. United States ex rel. Sanders*, 128 S. Ct. 2123 (June 9, 2008)

  - The Court held that a plaintiff asserting an FCA claim under the "false record or statement" section of the FCA (or a conspiracy claim based on same section) must prove that the defendant intended to cause a false claim to be paid by the Government, and not simply that the defendant intended to have a claim paid by a private entity using Government funds.

  - Defendant was a subcontractor that presented false records to the prime contractor to receive payment from the prime contractor

  - Court noted that FCA is not an "all-purpose anti-fraud statute"

- Original source – Rockwell Int'l Corp. v. United States, 127 S. Ct. 1397 (2007)

  - Relator was not an "original source" for purposes of the FCA because he did not have direct and independent knowledge of the facts alleged in his and the Government's joint amended complaint. Government recovery was based on later developed facts/theories

– Impact: Limits relators' ability to "piggyback" on fruits of Government investigations; relators will have to be more careful about what information goes into an amended complaint and what evidence is presented to the trier of fact

- Original source – U.S. *ex rel.* Richard Feingold v. Palmetto Gov't Benefits Adm'rs, 447 F. Supp. 2d 1187 (S.D. Fla. 2007)

  – Relator who never worked for the defendant, had no knowledge of the defendant's actual practices or procedures, and offered no evidence of false billing failed to plead fraud with the required particularity and was not an "original source" under the FCA because he relied solely on publicly available Medicare forms to proffer a variety of hypothetical arguments about how defendants must have falsified the information in them

- Presentment – U.S. *ex rel.* DRC, Inc v. Custer Battles, LLC, 472 F. Supp. 2d 787 (E.D. Va. 2007, 4th Cir. Appeal pending)

  – Allegedly false claims submitted by subcontractor to prime contractor do not violate FCA because sub's claims were never "presented" to the Government for payment, even though sub was paid by prime with monies through the Coalition Provisional Authority (CPA) partially funded by the U.S. Government

- Public Disclosure (Minority) – U.S. *ex rel.* Fowler v. Caremark RX, L.L.C., F.3d, 2007 WL 2142310 (C.A. 7 (Ill.))

  – In Fowler, the 7th Circuit reaffirmed its minority position that an action is based on publicly disclosed information if it both "depends on and is actually derived from publicly disclosed information"

- Public Disclosure (Majority) – U.S. *ex rel.* Boothe v. Sun Healthcare Group, Inc., F.3d, 2007 WL 2247666 (C.A. 10 (N.M.))

  – In Sun, the 10th Circuit found that an action is based on a public disclosure if it is "supported by" the public disclosure

- Recovery of FCA Defense Costs – The Boeing Co. v. Dep't of Energy, CBCA No. 337, July 9, 2007

  – A civil action under the FCA constitutes a fraud action within the meaning of contract clause providing that costs are unallowable if they are "incurred in defense of any civil or criminal fraud proceeding," making costs of defending an FCA action unallowable

- Release – U.S. *ex rel.* El-Amin v. George Washington Univ., 2007 WL 1302597 (D.D.C. 2007)

  – A release executed by a relator as part of an employment separation agreement without the Government's knowledge or consent, and which became effective before the Government had the opportunity to fully investigate the allegations, is unenforceable as against public policy

- What is a false claim/mistake – U.S. *ex rel.* Hefner v. Hackensack University Medical Center, 495 F.3d 103 (3rd Cir. 2007)

  – Absent a showing of reckless disregard or worse, mistaken double billings do not constitute false claims under the FCA

- What is a false claim/mistake – U.S. *ex rel.* Laird v. Lockheed Martin Eng'g & Sci. Servs. Co., 491 F.3d 254 (5th Cir. 2007)

  – Contractor did not violate FCA when it "underbid" a CPAF R&D contract because there was no evidence that the contractor did not intend to perform the contract according to the terms of its proposal or obtain payments to which it was not legitimately entitled, and the Government was partly responsible for the underbid because of unrealistic requirements

- Legislative Reaction – False Claims Act Correction Act of 2007

  – Senate version introduced on September 12, 2007 by Senators Grassley and Durbin and passed by Senate Judiciary Committee in April

    - Seeks to correct need to present claim to a federal Government agency or employee (renders *Allison Engine* & *Totten* decisions ineffective)

    - Amends FCA to eliminate a defendant's ability to seek dismissal of a *qui tam* claim in which the relator was not an original source of the information in the complaint (clear reaction to *Rockwell* decision)

    - Clarifies that false or fraudulent claims against non-US Government funds under control of US are subject to the FCA (renders *Custer Battles* decision ineffective) and proposes increased limitations period.

    - Government employee could act as *qui tam* relator if they had reported problem but no action taken within 12 months

  – House version introduced by Reps. Berman and Sensenbrenner in December would minimize pleading standard for a whistle-blowing plaintiff and make it difficult for a defendant to obtain a copy of the relator's disclosure statement to the Government in discovery

  – Still too early on to see where (if anywhere) this will go, but if passed it would significantly expand the scope of the FCA

Other Government Tools for Recovery

- *Daewoo*, 73 Fed. Cl. 547 (2006)

  – Government used Section 604 of the CDA to recover $50 million as a counterclaim to a claim filed by a contractor

- Court used a preponderance of evidence standard
- The Court also determined the contractor violated the FCA and other statutes and awarded nominal damages for these violations
- Clear Message – Don't inflate certified claims

- Forfeiture of Claims Act (25 U.S.C. sec. 2514)
  - Provides a claim shall be forfeited by any person who corruptly practices or attempts to practice any fraud against the US in the proof, statement, establishment or allowance thereof
  - Applies at the COFC only
  - Recent August 2007 Briefing Paper in this area

Suspension/Debarment

- The seeming sanction "*de jour*" in new legislation
- Arguably being used in a way that ignores fundamental purpose of suspension/debarment (*i.e.*, to protect the interests of the Government)
- GSA Inspector General activity
  - Seems to refer contractors for suspension and debarment relatively easily these days (*i.e.*, Navy boat barriers, Sun MAS contract pricing)
  - Always need to analyze impact that a settlement could have in this area
    - Show cause from "travel" matter settlement
- Expect further increase in activity in this area as more audits/investigations (from Iraqi contracting, etc.) develop
- Proposed Rulemaking and New Law

- Recent proposed FAR rule changes would impose suspension/debarment as penalty for knowing failure to timely disclose certain information to the Government, such as:

    - Overpayment on a contract

    - Violation of the FCA by a prime contractor or subcontractor

    - Violation of federal criminal law in connection with award or performance of a Government contract

- Sec. 6102 of the Emergency Military Supplemental Appropriations Act (H.R. 2642), signed into law on June 30, 2008, *requires* that the FAR be amended within 180 days to require timely notification by Federal contractors of overpayments or violations of federal criminal law on any contract valued >$5 million, including contracts for commercial items.

<u>Proposed Legislation</u>

- <u>The Border Control and Contractor Accountability Act of 2007 (HR 3496)</u>

    - Referred to Committee on Homeland Security on September 7, 2007

    - Legislation would debar or suspend contractors for three years if they or their subcontractors unlawfully employ aliens and for other purposes

    - Termination of contract unless the contractor agrees to terminate the alien's employment

    - Uses a preponderance of evidence standard

- <u>Defense Contracting Oversight Act of 2007 (HR 3383)</u>

- Referred to House Oversight and Government Reform Committee in August 2007

- DoD contractor must have internal ethics and compliance program in place within 30 days of contract award or face possible non-responsible finding

- Applies just to DoD contracts and contractors with $5 million in Government contract revenues the prior fiscal year

- A contractor may be suspended or debarred if it is determined that contractor personnel have not reported suspected improper conduct

• Defense Acquisition Reform Act of 2007 (S 32) (in committee)

  - Suspension and debarment of contractors that fails to report improper conduct

  - Limiting ability to increase costs on DoD contracts

  - Limiting award fee roll-overs and other changes

• Honest Leadership and Accountability in Contracting Act of 2007 (S 606) (in committee)

  - Suspension/debarment for pattern of overcharging the Government or for failing to comply with the law including tax, labor and employment, environmental, antitrust and consumer protection laws

  - In many ways, this is a reincarnation of the blacklisting rules that were defeated in 2000

• The Contractor and Federal Spending Accountability Act of 2007 (HR 3033) (passed by House and referred to Senate committtee)

  - Proposes to improve oversight of the suspension and debarment system for federal procurement contracts

- Provides for creation of a centralized database that documents and archives all civil, criminal, and administrative proceedings or complaints against any federal procurement or grant recipient in the past five years

- Requires any party applying for federal procurement or assistance to disclose any convictions or pending proceedings against the party involving any unethical activity associated with past Government contract work

- No party having two convictions, each constituting cause for debarment, within a three-year period involving similar infractions may be awarded any Government contracts or assistance

• FCPA Compliance Certification Legislation (HR 3405)

- Would require contractors to certify that there have been no violations of FCPA or be barred from being an offeror

- Would apply both to prime contracts and subcontracts at any tier

- No retroactive requirement, but also no time limitation as to the period covered by the required certification

- Similar proposed rulemaking in changes to FAR Case 2007-006 (*see* 73 Fed. Reg. 96 at 28407) would require contractor disclosure of known FCA violations

Other Procurement-Related Legislative Efforts

• Democrats taking control of Congress have led to increased oversight of agencies and their procurement policies, hearings and a host of proposed procurement-related legislation.

- Hearings include:

  • Iraq Reconstruction war profiteering

  - GSA schedule contract award and negotiation improprieties
  - Independence of Agency IGs
  - Increased competition and accountability

- Accountability in Government Contracting Act of 2007 (S 680)

  – Approved by unanimous Senate vote in November 2007, and referred to House for consideration

  – Require competition of all Government task or delivery orders over $100,000

  – Mandate post-award debriefs and allow protests for task or delivery orders over $5 million

  – Increase the amount of information required in a SOW for task and delivery orders over $5 million

  – Prohibit single awards of IDIQ contracts for services over $100 million

  – Clarify that the subpoena power of the IG extends to electronic documents

  – Allow designated federal entity IGs to investigate and report false claims and to recoup losses from fraud that do not exceed $150,000

  – Require the publication of all sole-source task or delivery orders above $100,000 within 10 business days of award

- Accountability in Contracting Act (HR 1362)

  – Similar to Senate version; passed House vote and referred to Senate

  – Of particular note is that this bill would also require disclosure of audit findings to Congress with no provisions for the protection of contractor proprietary information or for the contractor to receive notice or an opportunity to respond

- War Profiteering Prevention Act of 2007 (HR 400)

  - Passed by House and referred to Senate

  - Makes it a crime punishable up to 20 years and prison plus the greater of either $1 million or twice the gross profits of any person who willfully attempts or executes a scheme to defraud the US or materially overvalue any good or service with the specific intent to excessively profit from war, military action, or relief or reconstructions activities

  - Would apply outside the United States

  - Obvious reaction to perceived Iraq and Katrina reconstruction effort abuses

- The Commission on Wartime Contracting Act (S 1825)

  - Referred to House Committee on Homeland Security and Governmental Affairs

  - Establishes Commission on Wartime Contracting

  - Provides for study and investigation of wartime procurement contracts in Operation Iraqi Freedom and Operation Enduring Freedom

    - Commission would examine the effectiveness, extent of use, cost, etc. of wartime contracting

    - Additionally, the Commission would be responsible for investigating mismanagement and fraud associated with wartime procurement

    - Provides for the special IG for Iraq reconstruction to conduct audits in order to identify waste, fraud, mismanagement, etc.

Organizational Conflicts of Interest and Procurement Integrity Act Developments

- Increased scrutiny in areas of conflicts of interest (including OCI) and PIA violations (employment of former government personnel, etc.)

- Sec. 847 of FY2008 National Defense Authorization Act requires certain former DOD officials involved in large procurements (>$10 million) to obtain ethics letters prior to private employment.

- Probably still a reaction in many ways to recent high profile cases in this area

- We have seen greater IG subpoena/enforcement activity here

- "Revolving Door" changes proposed

  - Expanded definition of consultant to include lawyers and lobbyists

  - Longer duration (from one to two years)

- Recent OCI/False Claims Act decision (*U.S. v. Science Applications Int'l Corp.*, 2007 WL 2379735 (D.D.C. Aug. 22, 2007).

- Recent GAO Report on DOD personal conflicts of interest safeguards, due to blended workforce (GAO 08-169, March 2008)

- Need for clients to review policies procedures in this area to keep up with any changes

- Advance Notice of Proposed Rulemakings (FAR Cases 2007-017 and 2007-018) consider need for standard personal conflicts of interest clauses in Government contracts and standard OCI clauses in Solicitations that would extend to contractor employees

- Legislative developments

- Accountability in Government Contracting Act of 2007 (S 680) Possible OCI amendments to be added to the Accountability in Contracting Act

- The Executive Branch Reform Act of 2007 (HR 984) Impose restrictions aimed at "closing the revolving door" between Government and industry including a two year "cooling off" period

IRAQ Contracting Audit

- Massive Army audits of 18,000 Iraq contracts announced at end of August
- Army to comb through four years of contracts worth up to $3 billion for fraud, waste or abuse
- Audit will begin with office in Kuwait, which has been identified as a significant trouble spot
- KBR was only company specifically identified
- What next…?

Courtesy of Eric W. Leonard, Wiley Rein LLP

APPENDIX B

COMPLIANCE PLAN TABLE OF CONTENTS

A. Introduction

B. Basic Requirements for Government Contractors

1. Basic Contract Types
2. Commercial Contracts v. Federal Contracts
3. Governing Laws/Understanding the FAR

C. Integrity Issues

1. Improper Payments/Gifts
2. Procurement Integrity
3. Employment of Former Government Employees
4. Lobbying Restrictions/Political Activity
5. Suspended and Debarred Contractors
6. Conflicts of Interest
7. Contingent Fees
8. Antitrust/Bid Rigging Issues
9. Contact With Foreign Governments and Overseas Manufacturing
10. Sarbanes-Oxley Act

D. Communications with the Government

1. Representations and Certifications
2. False Statements
3. False Claims

E. Accounting and Financial Concerns for Government Contractors

1. Allowable Costs
2. Overhead Rates and Forward Pricing
3. Truth in Negotiations Act
4. Government Furnished Property
5. The Service Contract Act
6. Timekeeping Requirements

F. Socioeconomic Policies

1. Equal Employment Opportunity and Affirmative Action
2. Drug-Free Workplace

G. Information/Document Control and Retention for Government Contractors

1. Government-Provided Information
2. Security Classifications
3. Document Retention Requirements

H. Contract Performance Issues

1. Quality Control
2. Most Favored Customer Clauses
3. Submission of [Redacted] Information
4. Contract Claims
5. Change Orders
6. Export Control Laws

I. Government Audits and Investigations

1. Audits and Investigations
2. Obstruction of Justice

J. Reporting Violations

1. Employee Responsibility
2. Reporting Hotline
3. Non-Retaliation and Whistleblower Protections

K. Compliance and Discipline

L. Warning Signs

M. Quick Quiz

Acknowledgement of Receipt

Courtesy of Eric W. Leonard, Wiley Rein LLP

APPENDIX C

CONDUCTING BUSINESS IN THE FEDERAL GOVERNMENT MARKETPLACE

The Federal Government Marketplace

Overview

- Contracting with the Federal Government involves competing in a regulated marketplace and creates obligations and potential liabilities that generally do not exist in the commercial marketplace, including:
  - Limits on customer communication/interaction
  - Socioeconomic requirements
  - Longer term unpredictability
  - Potential criminalization of business disputes
  - Price justification and audits
- The existence of these Government-unique risks requires the establishment of oversight/compliance mechanisms within the company and associated internal structure
- *Reduced risks for "commercial item" contractor

Customer Communication/Interaction

Overview

- Competition for Federal contracts is a regulated process driven generally by concepts of equal opportunity, including:
  - Equal access to information
  - Publicly announced contract award criteria

- Enforcement of the competition rules through "bid protests"

– Many marketing/selling techniques that are normal in the commercial marketplace may create problems

– Training of sales force is necessary to alert them to the nuances of the Federal competition rules

<u>Gifts and Gratuities</u>

– It is a federal crime to provide a public official (1) anything of value (2) given, offered or promised (3) for or because of an official act performed, or to be performed by such public official

  - Tickets to events

  - Greens fees

  - Transportation

  - Meals

– Exceptions:

  - Modest items of food and refreshment

  - Gifts worth $20 or less, provided they do not exceed $50 per year

  - Items with little intrinsic value, *e.g.*, plaques, certificates

– Prime contractors may have similar policies prohibiting gifts/gratuities

<u>Anti-Kickback Act ("AKA")</u>

– Prohibits contractors from offering, soliciting, providing or accepting anything of value ***for the purpose of obtaining, or rewarding favorable treatment*** in connection with the award of a United States Government prime contract or subcontract.

– For example, cash, meals, trips, lodging, tickets to sporting events, loans, transportation, beverages, or personal services given to a customer in the federal marketplace in exchange for favorable treatment may be considered a violation.

Restrictions on Obtaining Competitor Information

– Federal law prohibits a company competing for the award of a contract from knowingly obtaining ***contractor bid proposal information*** before the award of a federal contract to which the information relates

– "Contractor bid or proposal information" includes:

- Cost or pricing data
- Portions of competitor's response to solicitations
- Information marked by the contractor as confidential or proprietary or otherwise marked as "contractor bid and proposal information"

– Federal law prohibits a company competing for the award of a contract from knowingly obtaining ***the Government's source selection information*** before the award of a federal contract to which the information relates

– "Source selection information" includes:

- Bid prices submitted to the Government
- Proposed costs or prices submitted to the Government
- Source selection plans
- Reports and evaluations of proposals
- Competitive range determinations
- Rankings of bids, proposals or competitors

- Other information marked "Source Selection Information"

Restrictions on Employment Discussions

– Discussions relating to future employment opportunities with current or former federal agency officials participating "personally and substantially" in procurements in excess of $100,000 where contractor is competing are restricted

– "One year ban" imposed for hiring certain former officials involved in procurements in excess of $10 million

Socioeconomic Requirements

Overview

– Special requirements for Federal contractors (and, in many instances, subcontractors) exist in areas such as:

  - Small and disadvantaged business preferences
  - Equal Opportunity/Affirmative Action
  - Labor standards
  - Buy American Act
  - Berry Amendment

– These requirements may require certifications of compliance and certain reporting obligations

– *Relaxed requirements for "commercial item" contractors

Small and Disadvantaged Business Preferences

– Government policy attempts to place a fair proportion of acquisitions with small business concerns and promote maximum subcontracting opportunities for small businesses

  - Set-asides

    - 8(a) program

    - Subcontracting goals/plans

- Additional preferences for women-owned, veteran-owned, and HUBZone small businesses

Equal Employment Opportunity/Affirmative Action

- It is the policy of contractor to afford equal employment opportunity to qualified individuals regardless of their race, color, religion, sex, national origin, age, or physical or mental handicap, and to comply with applicable laws and regulations

- Contractor is committed to promoting diversity in the workplace and is implementing an affirmative action program to increase minority representation at the contractor

- Workplace harassment in any manner or form is prohibited

Labor Standards

- Walsh-Healey Act requires contractors with Federal contracts in excess of $10,000 to manufacture or furnish materials, supplies, articles, and equipment to pay not less than the prevailing wage and to compensate employees at applicable overtime rates for work in excess of 40 hours in one week

- Service Contract Act applies to any Federal Government contract that exceeds $2,500 and whose principal purpose is to furnish services in the U.S. through the use of service employees and requires contractors to pay service employees not less than the prevailing wage and fringe benefits required to be paid for that locality

Buy American Act ("BAA")

- Restrictions on purchases of supplies that are foreign "end items" for use in the performance of Government contracts

- Articles, materials, and supplies acquired for Government contracts must be manufactured in the U.S. or comprised of "substantially all" domestic components (over 50% by cost)

  - For DOD, components may be domestic or from qualifying countries

- "Components" are materials and supplies incorporated directly into the end product – a foreign-made component may become domestic if it undergoes substantial manufacturing in the U.S.

The Berry Amendment

- Requires the DOD to give preference in procurement to domestically produced, manufactured, or home grown products

  - *E.g.*, food, clothing, specialty metals

- Specialty metals incorporated in products delivered under DOD contracts must be smelted in the U.S. or a "qualifying country"

- Specialty metals include certain steel, titanium, zirconium and other metal alloys that are important to the DOD

- Deviations permitted for certain electronic components procured under DOD contracts

Longer Term Unpredictability

Key Issues

- Federal appropriations laws generally limit the terms of contracts to one year

- Contractors must diligently protect IP rights in technical data and computer software via markings or risk losing some of those rights to the Government

- "Changes" clause contained in all contracts affords Government the unilateral right to make changes within the "general scope" of the contract, which may increase or decrease the cost of, or time required for, contract performance

- Different "changes" clause for "commercial item" contracts

– The "Termination for Convenience" (T/C) clause present in all contracts permits the Government to terminate contracts unilaterally for virtually any reason

– Contractors are entitled to receive an "equitable adjustment" to the contract for Changes and to be "made whole" financially in the event of a T/C, but a contractor may first be required to submit cost justifications and be subjected to a Government audit of the contractor's accounting records

- Mitigated risk for "commercial item" contractors

Potential Criminalization of Business Disputes

<u>Overview</u>

– Always a risk that business disputes arising from differing interpretations of contract requirements or contract negotiation tactics may generate a criminal investigation

– Even if outcome is ultimately favorable, investigations are inherently negative, unpleasant, and often very costly to defend

– Investigations may also raise the risk of debarment or suspension from Government contracting

<u>False Statement Act</u>

– Prohibits knowingly and willfully making a false statement concerning a matter within the jurisdiction of any department or agency of the United States

– Need not be directed to the government, *e.g.*, subcontractor invoice to prime qualifies

- Must be "material," but government need not rely on, be deceived by or be damaged by the statement

- The prohibition extends to both oral and written statements (sworn or unsworn), forms, certifications, invoices, letters, time cards, receipts and quotes

False Claims Act

- It is a crime to knowingly assert a false claim against the government

- A claim is a written demand or assertion seeking payment arising under or relating to a government contract

    - *E.g.*, invoice

- The claim need not be presented directly to the government to trigger the severe penalties associated with non-compliance

    - *E.g.*, false subcontractor invoice to prime

Price Justification and Audits

Overview

- Federal contracting officers (COs) must determine that the price of every contract the Government enters is "fair and reasonable"

- Determination is based, in many cases, on CO's analysis of contractor's certified "cost or pricing data," which includes all cost data (*e.g.*, labor/material costs and indirect/profit rates) in the contractor's possession related to the price proposed

- Submitted data must be certified as "accurate, current and complete," is subject to post-award audit for verification, and may create contractor liability for a retroactive "price reduction"

- However, in today's climate of "procurement reform" many of the risks and requirements associated with conducting business in the

Federal Marketplace have been reduced, particularly for vendors that provide "commercial items" under FAR Part 12

FAR Part 12 ("Commercial Items")

"Commercial Item" Contracting

Definition of a Commercial Item

- Products
  - "Of a type . . . customarily used" for "other than governmental purposes"
  - "Sold, leased or licensed"/offered for sale, lease or license to the "general public"
  - Even items "not yet available in the commercial marketplace"
- Modified Items
  - Modifications "of a type customarily available in the commercial marketplace"
  - "Minor" modifications to meet Government requirements
- Services
  - "Ancillary" services provided in support of a commercial product, *e.g.*, installation, maintenance, repair, training
  - "Pure" services "of a type offered and sold competitively in substantial quantities in the commercial marketplace"

Types of Contracts

- Cost reimbursement contracts prohibited
- Firm-fixed-price ("FFP") contracts or fixed-price contracts with economic price adjustment are the preferred vehicles for the acquisition of commercial items

- Time-and-materials ("T&M") or labor-hour ("LH") contracts permissible for acquisition of commercial services, under certain conditions

- Indefinite-delivery contracts if prices established based on a FFP, or rates are established for commercial services based on a T&M or LH basis

Benefits

- Simplified acquisition procedures for commercial item contracts > $5M

- No certified cost or pricing data under TINA

  - If necessary, CO may request "information other than cost and pricing data"

- Cost Accounting Standards ("CAS") does not apply

- Appropriate commercial practices incorporated

- Commercial terms and conditions ("Ts & Cs")

Key Ts & Cs

- "Changes" require mutual assent

- Contractor paid percentage of completion plus "reasonable charges" resulting from termination

  - No CAS or cost principles

  - Based on contractor's "standard record keeping system"

- Limited technical data rights for Government

- Limited required "flow downs"

- No Government audit rights

- Even with these relaxed requirements/obligations, oversight mechanisms and controls are needed to ensure continued compliance with applicable federal statutes and regulations

Recent Developments

- Increased criticism from various sources, including DOD Inspector General, regarding perceived inappropriate use of commercial item contracts

- DOD-proposed legislation would amend TINA to permit the Government to obtain certified cost and pricing data under certain conditions:

    - Insufficient commercial sales to determine price reasonableness

    - Prior submission by business segment

- Proposed FAR amendment would change "information other than cost or pricing data" to "data other than certified cost or pricing data"

    - Would permit COs to request "cost or pricing data" and "judgmental information" for certain commercial item contracts

- The House Armed Services Committee's FY '08 Defense Authorization Bill contains a number of provisions that would affect commercial item contracting

    - Remove "of a type" from definition of commercial services

    - Change TINA commercial item exception to allow CO to obtain certified cost or pricing data when a contract, subcontract, or modification for a commercial item is awarded noncompetitively

- Stay tuned …

FAR Part 15 Negotiated Contracts (Non-"Commercial Item" Contracting)

Non-"Commercial Item" Contracting

Overview

- Strict requirements concerning disclosure of contractors' cost and/or pricing data and accounting practices

- Truth in Negotiations Act ("TINA") requires submission of cost or pricing data and certification that data is accurate, complete, and current to ensure the Government is getting a fair and reasonable price

- Cost Accounting Standards ("CAS") regulate how costs are measured, assigned, and allocated

- Additional considerations

Truth in Negotiations Act ("TINA")

- Applies to awards/modifications ≥ $650K without sufficient competition to ensure price reasonableness, unless exception applies

- Requires submission of cost or pricing data, *i.e.*, factual information that a prudent buyer would expect to have a significant effect on price negotiations

- Contractors must certify that cost or pricing data are "accurate, current and complete" as of "shake hands date"

- Defective pricing could lead to price reduction, investigations/audits, and civil or criminal penalties

Cost Accounting Standards ("CAS")

- Applies to all negotiated Government contracts/subcontracts > $650K, unless the contract is exempt or a waiver is granted

- Varying types of CAS coverage depending on amount of award

- Requires contractors to disclose their cost accounting practices, follow their disclosed practices consistently, comply with CAS, and agree to an adjustment of the contract price if they fail to comply with CAS or follow disclosed practices

- CAS Board has the exclusive authority to make, promulgate, amend, and interpret CAS

Additional Considerations

- Increased audit exposure based on nature of work, *e.g.*, DCAA, agencies

- Need for more Government contract-specific processes and systems, *e.g.*, accounting system, and oversight mechanisms/centralized controls

- Special Prime Contractor considerations

    - Additional statutes and regulations

    - Possible need to develop purchasing and/or subcontract management systems

Courtesy of Eric W. Leonard, Wiley Rein LLP

APPENDIX D

FEDERAL ACQUISITION REGULATION, PART 27

PART 27 – PATENTS, DATA, AND COPYRIGHTS

27.000 Scope of Part.

This part prescribes the policies, procedures, solicitation provisions, and contract clauses pertaining to patents, data, and copyrights.

27.001 Definition.

"United States," as used in this part, means the 50 States and the District of Columbia, U.S. territories and possessions, Puerto Rico, and the Northern Mariana Islands.

Subpart 27.1 – GENERAL

27.101 Applicability.

This part applies to all agencies. However, agencies are authorized to adopt alternative policies, procedures, solicitation provisions, and contract clauses to the extent necessary to meet the specific requirements of laws, executive orders, treaties, or international agreements. Any agency adopting alternative policies, procedures, solicitation provisions, and contract clauses should include them in the agency's published regulations.

27.102 General Guidance.

(a) The Government encourages the maximum practical commercial use of inventions made under Government contracts.

(b) Generally, the Government will not refuse to award a contract on the grounds that the prospective contractor may infringe a patent. The Government may authorize and consent to the use of inventions in the performance of certain contracts, even though the inventions may be covered by U.S. patents.

(c) Generally, contractors providing commercial items should indemnify the Government against liability for the infringement of U.S. patents.

(d) The Government recognizes rights in data developed at private expense, and limits its demands for delivery of that data. When such data is delivered, the Government will acquire only those rights essential to its needs.

(e) Generally, the Government requires that contractors obtain permission from copyright owners before including copyrighted works, owned by others, in data to be delivered to the Government.

Subpart 27.2 – PATENTS AND COPYRIGHTS

27.200 Scope of Subpart.

This subpart prescribes policies and procedures with respect to –

(a) Patent and copyright infringement liability;

(b) Royalties;

(c) Security requirements for patent applications containing classified subject matter; and

(d) Patented technology under trade agreements.

27.201 Patent and Copyright Infringement Liability.

27.201-1 General

(a) Pursuant to 28 U.S.C. 1498, the exclusive remedy for patent or copyright infringement by or on behalf of the Government is a suit for monetary damages against the Government in the Court of Federal Claims. There is no injunctive relief available, and there is no direct cause of action against a contractor that is infringing a patent or copyright with the authorization or consent of the Government (e.g., while performing a contract).

(b) The Government may expressly authorize and consent to a contractor's use or manufacture of inventions covered by U.S. patents by inserting the clause at 52.227-1, Authorization and Consent.

(c) Because of the exclusive remedies granted in28 U.S.C. 1498, the Government requires notice and assistance from its contractors regarding any claims for patent or copyright infringement by inserting the clause at 52.227-2, Notice and Assistance, Regarding Patent and Copyright Infringement.

(d) The Government may require a contractor to reimburse it for liability for patent infringement arising out of a contract for commercial items by inserting the clause at FAR 52.227-3, Patent Indemnity.

27.201-2 Contract Clauses

(a)

(1) Insert the clause at 52.227-1, Authorization and Consent, in solicitations and contracts except that use of the clause is –

(i) Optional when using simplified acquisition procedures; and

(ii) Prohibited when both complete performance and delivery are outside the United States.

(2) Use the clause with its Alternate I in all R&D solicitations and contracts for which the primary purpose is R&D work, except that this alternate shall not be used in construction and architect-engineer contracts unless the contract calls exclusively for R&D work.

(3) Use the clause with its Alternate II in solicitations and contracts for communication services with a common carrier and the services are unregulated and not priced by a tariff schedule set by a regulatory body.

(b) Insert the clause at 52.227-2, Notice and Assistance Regarding Patent and Copyright Infringement, in all solicitations and contracts that include the clause at 52.227-1, Authorization and Consent.

(c)

(1) Insert the clause at 52.227-3, Patent Indemnity, in solicitations and contracts that may result in the delivery of commercial items, unless –

(i) Part 12 procedures are used;

(ii) The simplified acquisition procedures of Part 13 are used;

(iii) Both complete performance and delivery are outside the United States; or

(iv) The contracting officer determines after consultation with legal counsel that omission of the clause would be consistent with commercial practice.

(2) Use the clause with either its Alternate I (identification of excluded items) or II (identification of included items) if –

(i) The contract also requires delivery of items that are not commercial items; or

(ii) The contracting officer determines after consultation with legal counsel that limitation of applicability of the clause would be consistent with commercial practice.

(3) Use the clause with its Alternate III if the solicitation or contract is for communication services and facilities where performance is by a common carrier, and the services are unregulated and are not priced by a tariff schedule set by a regulatory body.

(d)

(1) Insert the clause at 52.227-4, Patent Indemnity – Construction Contracts, in solicitations and contracts for construction or that are fixed-price for dismantling, demolition, or removal of improvements. Do not insert the clause in contracts solely for architect-engineer services.

(2) If the contracting officer determines that the construction will necessarily involve the use of structures, products, materials, equipment, processes, or methods that are nonstandard, noncommercial, or special, the contracting officer may expressly exclude them from the patent indemnification by using the clause with its Alternate I. Note that this exclusion is for items, as distinguished from identified patents (see paragraph (e) of this subsection).

(e) It may be in the Government's interest to exempt specific U.S. patents from the patent indemnity clause. Exclusion from indemnity of identified patents, as distinguished from items, is the prerogative of the agency head. Upon written approval of the agency head, the contracting officer may insert the clause at 52.227-5, Waiver of Indemnity, in solicitations and contracts in addition to the appropriate patent indemnity clause.

(f) If a patent indemnity clause is not prescribed, the contracting officer may include one in the solicitation and contract if it is in the Government's interest to do so.

(g) The contracting officer shall not include in any solicitation or contract any clause whereby the Government agrees to indemnify a contractor for patent infringement.

27.202 Royalties.

27.202-1 Reporting of Royalties

(a) To determine whether royalties anticipated or actually paid under Government contracts are excessive, improper, or inconsistent with Government patent rights the solicitation provision at 52.227-6 requires prospective contractors to furnish royalty information. The contracting officer shall take appropriate action to reduce or eliminate excessive or improper royalties.

(b) If the response to a solicitation includes a charge for royalties, the contracting officer shall, before award of the contract, forward the information to the office having cognizance of patent matters for the contracting activity. The cognizant office shall promptly advise the contracting officer of appropriate action.

(c) The contracting officer, when considering the approval of a subcontract, shall require royalty information if it is required under the prime contract. The contracting officer shall forward the information to the office having cognizance of patent matters. However, the contracting officer need not delay consent while awaiting advice from the cognizant office.

(d) The contracting officer shall forward any royalty reports to the office having cognizance of patent matters for the contracting activity.

27.202-2 Notice of Government as a Licensee

(a) When the Government is obligated to pay a royalty on a patent because of an existing license agreement and the contracting officer believes that the licensed patent will be applicable to a prospective contract, the Government should furnish the prospective offerors with –

(1) Notice of the license;

(2) The number of the patent; and

(3) The royalty rate cited in the license.

(b) When the Government is obligated to pay such a royalty, the solicitation should also require offerors to furnish information indicating whether or not each offeror is the patent owner or a licensee under the patent. This information is necessary so that the Government may either –

(1) Evaluate an offeror's price by adding an amount equal to the royalty; or

(2) Negotiate a price reduction with an offeror when the offeror is licensed under the same patent at a lower royalty rate.

27.202-3 Adjustment of Royalties

(a) If at any time the contracting officer believes that any royalties paid, or to be paid, under a contract or subcontract are inconsistent with Government rights, excessive, or otherwise improper, the contracting officer shall promptly report the facts to the office having cognizance of patent matters for the contracting activity concerned.

(b) In coordination with the cognizant office, the contracting officer shall promptly act to protect the Government against payment of royalties –

(1) With respect to which the Government has a royalty-free license;

(2) At a rate in excess of the rate at which the Government is licensed; or

(3) When the royalties in whole or in part otherwise constitute an improper charge.

(c) In appropriate cases, the contracting officer in coordination with the cognizant office shall demand a refund pursuant to any refund of royalties clause in the contract (see 27.202-4) or negotiate for a reduction of royalties.

(d) For guidance in evaluating information furnished pursuant to 27.202-1, see 31.205-37. See also 31.109 regarding advance understandings on particular cost items, including royalties.

27.202-4 Refund of Royalties

The clause at 52.227-9, Refund of Royalties, establishes procedures to pay the contractor royalties under the contract and recover royalties not paid by the contractor when the royalties were included in the contractor's fixed price.

27.202-5 Solicitation Provisions and Contract Clause

(a)

(1) Insert a solicitation provision substantially the same as the provision at 52.227-6, Royalty Information, in –

(i) Any solicitation that may result in a negotiated contract for which royalty information is desired and for which cost or pricing data are obtained under 15.403; or

(ii) Sealed bid solicitations only if the need for such information is approved at a level above the contracting officer as being necessary for proper protection of the Government's interests.

(2) If the solicitation is for communication services and facilities by a common carrier, use the provision with its Alternate I.

(b) If the Government is obligated to pay a royalty on a patent involved in the prospective contract, insert in the solicitation a provision substantially the same as the provision at 52.227-7, Patents – Notice of Government Licensee. If the clause at 52.227-6 is not included in the solicitation, the contracting officer may require offerors to provide information sufficient to provide this notice to the other offerors.

(c) Insert the clause at 52.227-9, Refund of Royalties, in negotiated fixed-price solicitations and contracts when royalties may be paid under the contract. If a fixed-price incentive contract is contemplated, change "price" to "target cost and target profit" wherever it appears in the clause. The clause may be used in cost-reimbursement contracts where agency approval of royalties is necessary to protect the Government's interests.

27.203 Security Requirements for Patent Applications Containing Classified Subject Matter.

27.203-1 General

(a) Unauthorized disclosure of classified subject matter, whether in patent applications or resulting from the issuance of a patent, may be a violation of

18 U.S.C. 792, et seq. (Chapter 37 – Espionage and Censorship), and related statutes, and may be contrary to the interests of national security.

(b) Upon receipt of a patent application under paragraph (a) or (b) of the clause at 52.227-10, Filing of Patent Applications – Classified Subject Matter, the contracting officer shall ascertain the proper security classification of the patent application. If the application contains classified subject matter, the contracting officer shall inform the contractor how to transmit the application to the United States Patent Office in accordance with procedures provided by legal counsel. If the material is classified "Secret" or higher, the contracting officer shall make every effort to notify the contractor within 30 days of the Government's determination, pursuant to paragraph (a) of the clause.

(c) Upon receipt of information furnished by the contractor under paragraph (d) of the clause at 52.227-10, the contracting officer shall promptly submit that information to legal counsel in order that the steps necessary to ensure the security of the application will be taken.

(d) The contracting officer shall act promptly on requests for approval of foreign filing under paragraph (c) of the clause at 52.227-10 in order to avoid the loss of valuable patent rights of the Government or the contractor.

27.203-2 Contract Clause

Insert the clause at 52.227-10, Filing of Patent Applications – Classified Subject Matter, in all classified solicitations and contracts and in all solicitations and contracts where the nature of the work reasonably might result in a patent application containing classified subject matter.

27.204 Patented Technology Under Trade Agreements.

27.204-1 Use of Patented Technology Under the North American Free Trade Agreement

(a) The requirements of this section apply to the use of technology covered by a valid patent when the patent holder is from a country that is a party to the North American Free Trade Agreement (NAFTA).

(b) Article 1709(10) of NAFTA generally requires a user of technology covered by a valid patent to make a reasonable effort to obtain authorization prior to use of the patented technology. However, NAFTA provides that this requirement for authorization may be waived in situations of national emergency or other circumstances of extreme urgency, or for public noncommercial use.

(c) Section 6 of Executive Order 12889, "Implementation of the North American Free Trade Act," of December 27, 1993, waives the requirement to obtain advance authorization for an invention used or manufactured by or for the Federal Government. However, the patent owner shall be notified in advance whenever the agency or its contractor knows or has reasonable grounds to know, without making a patent search, that an invention described in and covered by a valid U.S. patent is or will be used or manufactured without a license. In cases of national emergency or other circumstances of extreme urgency, this notification need not be made in advance, but shall be made as soon as reasonably practicable.

(d) The contracting officer, in consultation with the office having cognizance of patent matters, shall ensure compliance with the notice requirements of NAFTA Article 1709(10) and Executive Order 12889. A contract award should not be suspended pending notification to the patent owner.

(e) Section 6(c) of Executive Order 12889 provides that the notice to the patent owner does not constitute an admission of infringement of a valid privately-owned patent.

(f) When addressing issues regarding compensation for the use of patented technology, Government personnel should be advised that NAFTA uses the term "adequate remuneration." Executive Order 12889 equates "remuneration" to "reasonable and entire compensation" as used in 28 U.S.C. 1498, the statute that gives jurisdiction to the U.S. Court of Federal Claims to hear patent and copyright cases involving infringement by the Government.

(g) When questions arise regarding the notice requirements or other matters relating to this section, the contracting officer should consult with legal counsel.

27.204-2 Use of Patented Technology Under the General Agreement on Tariffs and Trade (GATT)

Article 31 of Annex 1C, Agreement on Trade-Related Aspects of Intellectual Property Rights, to GATT (Uruguay Round) addresses situations where the law of a member country allows for use of a patent without authorization, including use by the Government.

Subpart 27.3 – PATENT RIGHTS UNDER GOVERNMENT CONTRACTS

27.300 Scope of Subpart.

This subpart prescribes policies, procedures, solicitation provisions, and contract clauses pertaining to inventions made in the performance of work under a Government contract or subcontract for experimental, developmental, or research work. Agency policies, procedures, solicitation provisions, and contract clauses may be specified in agency supplemental regulations as permitted by law, including 37 CFR 401.1.

27.301 Definitions.

As used in this subpart –

"Invention" means any invention or discovery that is or may be patentable or otherwise protectable under title 35 of the U.S. Code, or any variety of plant that is or may be protectable under the Plant Variety Protection Act (7 U.S.C. 2321, et seq.)

"Made" means –

> (1) When used in relation to any invention other than a plant variety, means the conception or first actual reduction to practice of the invention; or
>
> (2) When used in relation to a plant variety, means that the contractor has at least tentatively determined that the variety has been reproduced with recognized characteristics.

"Nonprofit organization" means a university or other institution of higher education or an organization of the type described in section 501(c)(3) of the Internal Revenue Code of 1954 (26 U.S.C. 501(c)) and exempt from taxation under section 501(a) of the Internal Revenue Code (26 U.S.C. 501(a)), or any nonprofit scientific or educational organization qualified under a State nonprofit organization statute.

"Practical application" means to manufacture, in the case of a composition or product; to practice, in the case of a process or method; or to operate, in the case of a machine or system; and, in each case, under such conditions as to establish that the invention is being utilized and that its benefits are, to the extent permitted by law or Government regulations, available to the public on reasonable terms.

"Subject invention" means any invention of the contractor made in the performance of work under a Government contract.

27.302 Policy.

(a) Introduction. In accordance with chapter 18 of title 35, U.S.C. (as implemented by 37 CFR part 401), Presidential Memorandum on Government Patent Policy to the Heads of Executive Departments and Agencies dated February 18, 1983, and Executive Order 12591, Facilitating Access to Science and Technology dated April 10, 1987, it is the policy and objective of the Government to –

> (1) Use the patent system to promote the use of inventions arising from federally supported research or development;
>
> (2) Encourage maximum participation of industry in federally supported research and development efforts;
>
> (3) Ensure that these inventions are used in a manner to promote free competition and enterprise without unduly encumbering future research and discovery;
>
> (4) Promote the commercialization and public availability of the inventions made in the United States by United States industry and labor;

(5) Ensure that the Government obtains sufficient rights in federally supported inventions to meet the needs of the Government and protect the public against nonuse or unreasonable use of inventions; and

(6) Minimize the costs of administering patent policies.

(b) Contractor right to elect title.

(1) Generally, pursuant to 35 U.S.C. 202 and the Presidential Memorandum and Executive order cited in paragraph (a) of this section, each contractor may, after required disclosure to the Government, elect to retain title to any subject invention.

(2) A contract may require the contractor to assign to the Government title to any subject invention –

(i) When the contractor is not located in the United States or does not have a place of business located in the United States or is subject to the control of a foreign government (see 27.303 (e)(1)(i));

(ii) In exceptional circumstances, when an agency determines that restriction or elimination of the right to retain title in any subject invention will better promote the policy and objectives of chapter 18 of title 35, U.S.C. and the Presidential Memorandum;

(iii) When a Government authority, that is authorized by statute or executive order to conduct foreign intelligence or counterintelligence activities, determines that the restriction or elimination of the right to retain title to any subject invention is necessary to protect the security of such activities;

(iv) When the contract includes the operation of a Government-owned, contractor-operated facility of the Department of Energy (DOE) primarily dedicated to the Department's naval nuclear propulsion or weapons related programs and all funding agreement limitations under 35

U.S.C. 202(a)(iv) for agreements with small business concerns and nonprofit organizations are limited to inventions occurring under the above two programs; or

(v) Pursuant to statute or in accordance with agency regulations.

(3) When the Government has the right to acquire title to a subject invention, the contractor may, nevertheless, request greater rights to a subject invention (see 27.304-1(c)).

(4) Consistent with 37 CFR part 401, when a contract with a small business concern or nonprofit organization requires assignment of title to the Government based on the exceptional circumstances enumerated in paragraph (b)(2)(ii) or (iii) of this section for reasons of national security, the contract shall still provide the contractor with the right to elect ownership to any subject invention that –

(i) Is not classified by the agency; or

(ii) Is not limited from dissemination by the DOE within 6 months from the date it is reported to the agency.

(5) Contracts in support of DOE's naval nuclear propulsion program are exempted from this paragraph (b).

(6) When a contract involves a series of separate task orders, an agency may structure the contract to apply the exceptions at paragraph (b)(2)(ii) or (iii) of this section to individual task orders.

(c) Government license. The Government shall have at least a nonexclusive, nontransferable, irrevocable, paid-up license to practice, or have practiced for or on behalf of the United States, any subject invention throughout the world. The Government may require additional rights in order to comply with treaties or other international agreements. In such case, these rights shall be made a part of the contract (see 27.303).

(d) Government right to receive title.

(1) In addition to the right to obtain title to subject inventions pursuant to paragraph (b)(2)(i) through (v) of this section, the Government has the right to receive title to an invention –

(i) If the contractor has not disclosed the invention within the time specified in the clause; or

(ii) In any country where the contractor –

(A) Does not elect to retain rights or fails to elect to retain rights to the invention within the time specified in the clause;

(B) Has not filed a patent or plant variety protection application within the time specified in the clause;

(C) Decides not to continue prosecution of a patent or plant variety protection application, pay maintenance fees, or defend in a reexamination or opposition proceeding on the patent; or

(D) No longer desires to retain title.

(2) For the purposes of this paragraph, filing in a European Patent Office Region or under the Patent Cooperation Treaty constitutes election in the countries selected in the application(s).

(e) Utilization reports. The Government has the right to require periodic reporting on how any subject invention is being used by the contractor or its licensees or assignees. In accordance with 35 U.S.C. 202(c)(5) and 37 CFR part 401, agencies shall not disclose such utilization reports to persons outside the Government without permission of the contractor. Contractors should mark as confidential/proprietary any utilization report to help prevent inadvertent release outside the Government.

(f) March-in rights.

(1) Pursuant to 35 U.S.C. 203, agencies have certain march-in rights that require the contractor, an assignee, or exclusive licensee of a

subject invention to grant a nonexclusive, partially exclusive, or exclusive license in any field of use to responsible applicants, upon terms that are reasonable under the circumstances. If the contractor, assignee or exclusive licensee of a subject invention refuses to grant such a license, the agency can grant the license itself. March-in rights may be exercised only if the agency determines that this action is necessary –

(i) Because the contractor or assignee has not taken, or is not expected to take within a reasonable time, effective steps to achieve practical application of the subject invention in the field(s) of use;

(ii) To alleviate health or safety needs that are not reasonably satisfied by the contractor, assignee, or their licensees;

(iii) To meet requirements for public use specified by Federal regulations and these requirements are not reasonably satisfied by the contractor, assignee, or licensees; or

(iv) Because the agreement required by paragraph (g) of this section has neither been obtained nor waived, or because a licensee of the exclusive right to use or sell any subject invention in the United States is in breach of its agreement obtained pursuant to paragraph (g) of this section.

(2) The agency shall not exercise its march-in rights unless the contractor has been provided a reasonable time to present facts and show cause why the proposed agency action should not be taken. The agency shall provide the contractor an opportunity to dispute or appeal the proposed action, in accordance with 27.304-1 (g).

(g) Preference for United States industry. In accordance with 35 U.S.C. 204, no contractor that receives title to any subject invention and no assignee of the contractor shall grant to any person the exclusive right to use or sell any subject invention in the United States unless that person agrees that any products embodying the subject invention or produced through the use of the subject invention will be manufactured substantially in the United States. However, in individual cases, the requirement for this agreement may be waived by the agency upon a showing by the contractor or assignee that reasonable but unsuccessful efforts have been made to grant licenses on similar terms to potential licensees that would be likely to manufacture substantially in the United States or that under the circumstances domestic manufacture is not commercially feasible.

(h) Special conditions for nonprofit organizations' preference for small business concerns.

> (1) Nonprofit organization contractors are expected to use reasonable efforts to attract small business licensees (see paragraph (i)(4) of the clause at 52.227-11, Patent Rights – Ownership by the Contractor). What constitutes reasonable efforts to attract small business licensees will vary with the circumstances and the nature, duration, and expense of efforts needed to bring the invention to the market.
>
> (2) Small business concerns that believe a nonprofit organization is not meeting its obligations under the clause may report the matter to the Secretary of Commerce. To the extent deemed appropriate, the Secretary of Commerce will undertake informal investigation of the matter, and may discuss or negotiate with the nonprofit organization ways to improve its efforts to meet its obligations under the clause. However, in no event will the Secretary of Commerce intervene in ongoing negotiations or contractor decisions concerning the licensing of a specific subject invention. These investigations, discussions, and negotiations involving the Secretary of Commerce will be in coordination with other interested agencies, including the Small Business Administration. In the case of a contract for the operation of a Government-owned, contractor-operated research or production facility, the Secretary of Commerce will coordinate with the agency responsible for the facility prior to any discussions or negotiations with the contractor.

(i) Minimum rights to contractor.

(1) When the Government acquires title to a subject invention, the contractor is normally granted a revocable, nonexclusive, paid-up license to that subject invention throughout the world. The contractor's license extends to any of its domestic subsidiaries and affiliates within the corporate structure of which the contractor is a part and includes the right to grant sublicenses to the extent the contractor was legally obligated to do so at the time of contract award. The contracting officer shall approve or disapprove, in writing, any contractor request to transfer its licenses. No approval is necessary when the transfer is to the successor of that part of the contractor's business to which the subject invention pertains.

(2) In response to a third party's proper application for an exclusive license, the contractor's domestic license may be revoked or modified to the extent necessary to achieve expeditious practical application of the subject invention. The application shall be submitted in accordance with the applicable provisions in 37 CFR part 404 and agency licensing regulations. The contractor's license will not be revoked in that field of use or the geographical areas in which the contractor has achieved practical application and continues to make the benefits of the subject invention reasonably accessible to the public. The license in any foreign country may be revoked or modified to the extent the contractor, its licensees, or its domestic subsidiaries or affiliates have failed to achieve practical application in that country. (See the procedures at 27.304(f).)

(j) Confidentiality of inventions. Publishing information concerning an invention before a patent application is filed on a subject invention may create a bar to a valid patent. To avoid this bar, agencies may withhold information from the public that discloses any invention in which the Government owns or may own a right, title, or interest (including a nonexclusive license) (see 35 U.S.C. 205 and 37 CFR part 401). Agencies may only withhold information concerning inventions for a reasonable time in order for a patent application to be filed. Once filed in any patent office, agencies are not required to release copies of any document that is a part of a patent application for those subject inventions. (See also 27.305-4.)

27.303 Contract Clauses.

(a)

(1) Insert a patent rights clause in all solicitations and contracts for experimental, developmental, or research work as prescribed in this section.

(2) This section also applies to solicitations or contracts for construction work or architect-engineer services that include –

(i) Experimental, developmental, or research work;

(ii) Test and evaluation studies; or

(iii) The design of a Government facility that may involve novel structures, machines, products, materials, processes, or equipment (including construction equipment).

(3) The contracting officer shall not include a patent rights clause in solicitations or contracts for construction work or architect-engineer services that call for or can be expected to involve only "standard types of construction" "Standard types of construction" are those involving previously developed equipment, methods, and processes and in which the distinctive features include only –

(i) Variations in size, shape, or capacity of conventional structures; or

(ii) Purely artistic or aesthetic (as distinguished from functionally significant) architectural configurations and designs of both structural and nonstructural members or groupings, whether or not they qualify for design patent protection.

(b)

(1) Unless an alternative patent rights clause is used in accordance with paragraph (c), (d), or (e) of this section, insert the clause at 52.227-11, Patent Rights – Ownership by the Contractor.

(2) To the extent the information is not required elsewhere in the contract, and unless otherwise specified by agency supplemental regulations, the contracting officer may modify 52.227-11 (e) or otherwise supplement the clause to require the contractor to do one or more of the following:

(i) Provide periodic (but not more frequently than annually) listings of all subject inventions required to be disclosed during the period covered by the report.

(ii) Provide a report prior to the closeout of the contract listing all subject inventions or stating that there were none.

(iii) Provide the filing date, serial number, title, patent number and issue date for any patent application filed on any subject invention in any country or, upon request, copies of any patent application so identified.

(iv) Furnish the Government an irrevocable power to inspect and make copies of the patent application file when a Government employee is a co-inventor.

(3) Use the clause with its Alternate I if the Government must grant a foreign government a sublicense in subject inventions pursuant to a specified treaty or executive agreement. The contracting officer may modify Alternate I, if the agency head determines, at contract award, that it would be in the national interest to sublicense foreign governments or international organizations pursuant to any existing or future treaty or agreement. When necessary to effectuate a treaty or agreement, Alternate I may be appropriately modified.

(4) Use the clause with its Alternate II in contracts that may be affected by existing or future treaties or agreements.

(5) Use the clause with its Alternate III in contracts with nonprofit organizations for the operation of a Government-owned facility.

(6) If the contract is for the operation of a Government-owned facility, the contracting officer may use the clause with its Alternate IV.

(7) If the contract is for the performance of services at a Government owned and operated laboratory or at a Government owned and contractor operated laboratory directed by the Government to fulfill the Government's obligations under a Cooperative Research and Development Agreement (CRADA) authorized by 15 U.S.C. 3710a, the contracting officer may use the clause with its Alternate V. Since this provision is considered an exercise of an agency's "exceptional circumstances" authority, the contracting officer must comply with 37 CFR 401.3(e) and 401.4.

(c) Insert a patent rights clause in accordance with the procedures at 27.304-2 if the solicitation or contract is being placed on behalf of another Government agency.

(d) Insert a patent rights clause in accordance with agency procedures if the solicitation or contract is for DoD, DOE, or NASA, and the contractor is other than a small business concern or nonprofit organization.

(e)

(1) Except as provided in paragraph (e)(2) of this section, and after compliance with the applicable procedures in 27.304-1(b), the contracting officer may insert the clause at 52.227-13, Patent Rights – Ownership by the Government, or a clause prescribed by agency supplemental regulations, if –

(i) The contractor is not located in the United States or does not have a place of business located in the United States or is subject to the control of a foreign government;

(ii) There are exceptional circumstances and the agency head determines that restriction or elimination of the right to retain title to any subject invention will better promote the policy and objectives of chapter 18 of title 35 of the United States Code;

(iii) A Government authority that is authorized by statute or executive order to conduct foreign intelligence or counterintelligence activities, determines that restriction or elimination of the right to retain any subject invention is necessary to protect the security of such activities; or

(iv) The contract includes the operation of a Government-owned, contractor-operated facility of DOE primarily dedicated to that Department's naval nuclear propulsion or weapons related programs.

(2) If an agency exercises the exceptions at paragraph (e)(1)(ii) or (iii) of this section in a contract with a small business concern or a nonprofit organization, the contracting officer shall use the clause at 52.227-11 with only those modifications necessary to address the exceptional circumstances and shall include in the modified clause greater rights determinations procedures equivalent to those at 52.227-13(b)(2).

(3) When using the clause at 52.227-13, Patent Rights – Ownership by the Government, the contracting officer may supplement the clause to require the contractor to –

(i) Furnish a copy of each subcontract containing a patent rights clause (but if a copy of a subcontract is furnished under another clause, a duplicate shall not be requested under the patent rights clause);

(ii) Submit interim and final invention reports listing subject inventions and notifying the contracting officer of all subcontracts awarded for experimental, developmental, or research work;

(iii) Provide the filing date, serial number, title, patent number, and issue date for any patent application filed on any subject invention in any country or, upon specific request, copies of any patent application so identified; and

(iv) Submit periodic reports on the utilization of a subject invention.

(4) Use the clause at 52.227-13 with its Alternate I if –

(i) The Government must grant a foreign government a sublicense in subject inventions pursuant to a treaty or executive agreement; or

(ii) The agency head determines, at contract award, that it would be in the national interest to sublicense foreign governments or international organizations pursuant to any existing or future treaty or agreement. If other rights are necessary to effectuate any treaty or agreement, Alternate I may be appropriately modified.

(5) Use the clause at 52.227-13 with its Alternate II in the contract when necessary to effectuate an existing or future treaty or agreement.

27.304 Procedures.

27.304-1 General

(a) Status as small business concern or nonprofit organization. If an agency has reason to question the size or nonprofit status of the prospective contractor, the agency may require the prospective contractor to furnish evidence of its nonprofit status or may file a size protest in accordance with FAR 19.302.

(b) Exceptions.

(1) Before using any of the exceptions under 27.303(e)(1) in a contract with a small business concern or a nonprofit organization and before using the exception of 27.303(e)(1)(ii) for any contractor, the agency shall follow the applicable procedures at 37 CFR 401.

(2) A small business concern or nonprofit organization is entitled to an administrative review of the use of the exceptions at

27.303(e)(1)(i) through (e)(1)(iv) in accordance with agency procedures and 37 CFR part 401.

(c) Greater rights determinations. Whenever the contract contains the clause at 52.227-13, Patent Rights – Ownership by the Government, or a patent rights clause modified pursuant to 27.303(e)(2), the contractor (or an employee-inventor of the contractor after consultation with the contractor) may request greater rights to an identified invention within the period specified in the clause. The contracting officer may grant requests for greater rights if the contracting officer determines that the interests of the United States and the general public will be better served. In making these determinations, the contracting officer shall consider at least the following objectives (see 37 CFR 401.3(b) and 401.15):

(1) Promoting the utilization of inventions arising from federally supported research and development.

(2) Ensuring that inventions are used in a manner to promote full and open competition and free enterprise without unduly encumbering future research and discovery.

(3) Promoting public availability of inventions made in the United States by United States industry and labor.

(4) Ensuring that the Government obtains sufficient rights in federally supported inventions to meet the needs of the Government and protect the public against nonuse or unreasonable use of inventions.

(d) Retention of rights by inventor. If the contractor elects not to retain title to a subject invention, the agency may consider and, after consultation with the contractor, grant requests for retention of rights by the inventor. Retention of rights by the inventor will be subject to the conditions in paragraphs (d) (except paragraph (d)(1)(i)), (e)(4), (f), (g), and (h) of the clause at 52.227-11, Patent Rights – Ownership by the Contractor.

(e) Government assignment to contractor of rights in Government employees' inventions. When a Government employee is a co-inventor of an invention made under a contract with a small business concern or nonprofit organization, the agency employing the co-inventor may license or assign whatever rights it may acquire in the subject invention from its employee to the contractor, subject at least to the conditions of 35 U.S.C. 202-204.

(f) Revocation or modification of contractor's minimum rights. Before revoking or modifying the contractor's license in accordance with 27.302(i)(2), the contracting officer shall furnish the contractor a written notice of intention to revoke or modify the license. The agency shall allow the contractor at least 30 days (or another time as may be authorized for good cause by the contracting officer) after the notice to show cause why the license should not be revoked or modified. The contractor has the right to appeal, in accordance with applicable regulations in 37 CFR part 404 and agency licensing regulations, any decisions concerning the revocation or modification.

(g) Exercise of march-in rights. When exercising march-in rights, agencies shall follow the procedures set forth in 37 CFR 401.6.

(h) Licenses and assignments under contracts with nonprofit organizations. If the contractor is a nonprofit organization, paragraph (i) of the clause at 52.227-11 provides that certain contractor actions require agency approval.

27.304-2 Contracts Placed by or for Other Government Agencies

The following procedures apply unless an interagency agreement provides otherwise:

(a) When a Government agency requests another Government agency to award a contract on its behalf, the request should explain any special circumstances surrounding the contract and specify the patent rights clause to be used. The clause should be selected and modified, if necessary, in accordance with the policies and procedures of this subpart. If, however, the request states that a clause of the requesting agency is required (e.g., because of statutory requirements, a deviation, or exceptional circumstances), the awarding agency shall use that clause rather than those of this subpart.

(1) If the request states that an agency clause is required and the work to be performed under the contract is not severable and is funded wholly or in part by the requesting agency, then include the requesting agency clause and no other patent rights clause in the contract.

(2) If the request states that an agency clause is required, and the work to be performed under the contract is severable, then the contracting officer shall assure that the requesting agency clause applies only to that severable portion of the work and that the work for the awarding agency is subject to the appropriate patent rights clause.

(3) If the request states that a requesting agency clause is not required in any resulting contract, the awarding agency shall use the appropriate patent rights clause, if any.

(b) Any action requiring an agency determination, report, or deviation involved in the use of the requesting agency's clause is the responsibility of the requesting agency unless the agencies agree otherwise. However, the awarding agency may not alter the requesting agency's clause without prior approval of the requesting agency.

(c) The requesting agency may require, and provide instructions regarding, the forwarding or handling of any invention disclosures or other reporting requirements of the specified clauses. Normally, the requesting agency is responsible for the administration of any subject inventions. This responsibility shall be established in advance of awarding any contracts.

27.304-3 Subcontracts

(a) The policies and procedures in this subpart apply to all subcontracts at any tier.

(b) Whenever a prime contractor or a subcontractor considers including a particular clause in a subcontract to be inappropriate or a subcontractor refuses to accept the clause, the contracting officer, in consultation with counsel, shall resolve the matter.

(c) It is Government policy that contractors shall not use their ability to award subcontracts as economic leverage to acquire rights for themselves in inventions resulting from subcontracts.

27.304-4 Appeals

(a) The designated agency official shall provide the contractor with a written statement of the basis, including any relevant facts, for taking any of the following actions:

> (1) A refusal to grant an extension to the invention disclosure period under paragraph (c)(4) of the clause at 52.227-11;
>
> (2) A demand for a conveyance of title to the Government under 27.302(d)(1)(i) and (ii);
>
> (3) A refusal to grant a waiver under 27.302(g), Preference for United States industry; or
>
> (4) A refusal to approve an assignment under 27.304-1(h).

(b) Each agency may establish and publish procedures under which any of these actions may be appealed. These appeal procedures should include administrative due process procedures and standards for fact-finding. The resolution of any appeal shall consider both the factual and legal basis for the action and its consistency with the policy and objectives of 35 U.S.C. 200-206 and 210.

(c) To the extent that any of the actions described in paragraph (a) of this section are subject to appeal under the Contract Disputes Act, the procedures under that Act will satisfy the requirements of paragraph (b).

27.305 Administration of Patent Rights Clauses.

27.305-1 Goals

(a) Contracts having a patent rights clause should be so administered that –

> (1) Inventions are identified, disclosed, and reported as required by the contract, and elections are made;

(2) The rights of the Government in subject inventions are established;

(3) When patent protection is appropriate, patent applications are timely filed and prosecuted by contractors or by the Government;

(4) The rights of the Government in filed patent applications are documented by formal instruments such as licenses or assignments; and

(5) Expeditious commercial utilization of subject inventions is achieved.

(b) If a subject invention is made under a contract funded by more than one agency, at the request of the contractor or on their own initiative, the agencies shall designate one agency as responsible for administration of the rights of the Government in the invention.

27.305-2 Administration by the Government

(a) Agencies should establish and maintain appropriate follow-up procedures to protect the Government's interest and to check that subject inventions are identified and disclosed, and when appropriate, patent applications are filed, and that the Government's rights therein are established and protected. Follow-up activities for contracts that include a clause referenced in 27.304-2 should be coordinated with the appropriate agency.

(b)

(1) The contracting officer administering the contract (or other representative specifically designated in the contract for this purpose) is responsible for receiving invention disclosures, reports, confirmatory instruments, notices, requests, and other documents and information submitted by the contractor pursuant to a patent rights clause.

(i) For other than confirmatory instruments, if the contractor fails to furnish documents or information as called for by the clause within the time required, the contracting officer shall promptly request the contractor to supply the required documents or information. If the failure persists, the contracting officer shall take appropriate action to secure compliance.

(ii) If the contractor does not furnish confirmatory instruments within 6 months after filing each patent application, or within 6 months after submitting the invention disclosure if the application has been previously filed, the contracting officer shall request the contractor to supply the required documents.

(2) The contracting officer shall promptly furnish all invention disclosures, reports, confirmatory instruments, notices, requests, and other documents and information relating to patent rights clauses to legal counsel.

(c) Contracting activities should establish appropriate procedures to detect and correct failures by the contractor to comply with its obligations under the patent rights clauses, such as failures to disclose and report subject inventions, both during and after contract performance. Government effort to review and correct contractor compliance with its patent rights obligations should be directed primarily toward contracts that are more likely to result in subject inventions significant in number or quality. These contracts include contracts of a research, developmental, or experimental nature; contracts of a large dollar amount; and any other contracts when there is reason to believe the contractor may not be complying with its contractual obligations. Other contracts may be reviewed using a spot-check method, as feasible. Appropriate follow-up procedures and activities may include the investigation or review of selected contracts or contractors by those qualified in patent and technical matters to detect failures to comply with contract obligations.

(d) Follow-up activities should include, where appropriate, use of Government patent personnel –

(1) To interview agency technical personnel to identify novel developments made in contracts;

(2) To review technical reports submitted by contractors with cognizant agency technical personnel;

(3) To check the Official Gazette of the United States Patent and Trademark Office and other sources for patents issued to the contractor in fields related to its Government contracts; and

(4) To have cognizant Government personnel interview contractor personnel regarding work under the contract involved, observe the work on site, and inspect laboratory notebooks and other records of the contractor related to work under the contract.

(e) If a contractor or subcontractor does not have a clear understanding of its obligations under the clause, or its procedures for complying with the clause are deficient, the contracting officer should explain to the contractor its obligations. The withholding of payments provision (if any) of the patent rights clause may be invoked if the contractor fails to meet the obligations required by the patents rights clause. Significant or repeated failures by a contractor to comply with the patent rights obligation in its contracts shall be documented and made a part of the general file (see 4.801(c)(3)).

27.305-3 Securing Invention Rights Acquired by the Government

(a) Agencies are responsible for implementing procedures necessary to protect the Government's interest in subject inventions. When the Government acquires the entire right, title, and interest in an invention by contract, the chain of title from the inventor to the Government shall be clearly established. This is normally accomplished by an assignment either from each inventor to the contractor and from the contractor to the Government, or from the inventor to the Government with the consent of the contractor. When the Government's rights are limited to a license, there should be a confirmatory instrument to that effect.

(b) Agencies may, by supplemental instructions, develop suitable assignments, licenses, and other papers evidencing any rights of the Government in patents or patents applications. These instruments should be recorded in the U.S. Patent and Trademark Office (see Executive Order 9424, Establishing in the United States Patent Office a Register of

Government Interests in Patents and Applications for Patents, (February 18, 1944).

27.305-4 Protection of Invention Disclosures

(a) The Government will, to the extent authorized by 35 U.S.C. 205, withhold from disclosure to the public any invention disclosures reported under the patent rights clauses of 52.227-11 or 52.227-13 for a reasonable time in order for patent applications to be filed. The Government will follow the policy in 27.302(j) regarding protection of confidentiality.

(b) The Government should also use reasonable efforts to withhold from disclosure to the public for a reasonable time other information disclosing a subject invention. This information includes any data delivered pursuant to contract requirements provided that the contractor notifies the agency as to the identity of the data and the subject invention to which it relates at the time of delivery of the data. This notification shall be provided to both the contracting officer and to any patent representative to which the invention is reported, if other than the contracting officer.

(c) For more information on protection of invention disclosures, also see 37 CFR 401.13.

27.306 Licensing Background Patent Rights to Third Parties.

(a) A contract with a small business concern or nonprofit organization shall not contain a provision allowing the Government to require the licensing to third parties of inventions owned by the contractor that are not subject inventions unless the agency head has approved and signed a written justification in accordance with paragraph (b) of this section. The agency head may not delegate this authority and may exercise the authority only if it is determined that the –

> (1) Use of the invention by others is necessary for the practice of a subject invention or for the use of a work object of the contract; and
>
> (2) Action is necessary to achieve the practical application of the subject invention or work object.

(b) Any determination will be on the record after an opportunity for a hearing, and the agency shall notify the contractor of the determination by certified or registered mail. The notification shall include a statement that the contractor must bring any action for judicial review of the determination within 60 days after the notification.

Subpart 27.4 – RIGHTS IN DATA AND COPYRIGHTS

27.400 Scope of Subpart.

This subpart sets forth policies and procedures regarding rights in data and copyrights, and acquisition of data. The policy statement in 27.402 applies to all executive agencies. The remainder of the subpart applies to all executive agencies except the Department of Defense.

27.401 Definitions.

As used in this subpart –

"Data" means recorded information, regardless of form or the media on which it may be recorded. The term includes technical data and computer software. The term does not include information incidental to contract administration, such as financial, administrative, cost or pricing, or management information.

"Form, fit, and function data" means data relating to items, components, or processes that are sufficient to enable physical and functional interchangeability, and data identifying source, size, configuration, mating and attachment characteristics, functional characteristics, and performance requirements. For computer software it means data identifying source, functional characteristics, and performance requirements, but specifically excludes the source code, algorithms, processes, formulas, and flow charts of the software.

"Limited rights" means the rights of the Government in limited rights data as set forth in a Limited Rights Notice.

"Limited rights data" means data, other than computer software, that embody trade secrets or are commercial or financial and confidential or privileged, to the extent that such data pertain to items, components, or processes developed at private expense, including minor modifications. (Agencies may, however, adopt the following alternate definition: Limited rights data means data (other than computer software) developed at private expense that embody trade secrets or are commercial or financial and confidential or privileged (see 27.404-2(b)).

"Restricted computer software" means computer software developed at private expense and that is a trade secret, is commercial or financial and confidential or privileged, or is copyrighted computer software, including minor modifications of the computer software.

"Restricted rights" means the rights of the Government in restricted computer software as set forth in a Restricted Rights Notice.

"Unlimited rights" means the rights of the Government to use, disclose, reproduce, prepare derivative works, distribute copies to the public, and perform publicly and display publicly, in any manner and for any purpose, and to have or permit others to do so.

27.402 Policy.

(a) To carry out their missions and programs, agencies acquire or obtain access to many kinds of data produced during or used in the performance of their contracts. Agencies require data to –

(1) Obtain competition among suppliers;

(2) Fulfill certain responsibilities for disseminating and publishing the results of their activities;

(3) Ensure appropriate utilization of the results of research, development, and demonstration activities including the dissemination of technical information to foster subsequent technological developments;

(4) Meet other programmatic and statutory requirements; and

(5) Meet specialized acquisition needs and ensure logistics support.

(b) Contractors may have proprietary interests in data. In order to prevent the compromise of these interests, agencies shall protect proprietary data from unauthorized use and disclosure. The protection of such data is also necessary to encourage qualified contractors to participate in and apply innovative concepts to Government programs. In light of these considerations, agencies shall balance the Government's needs and the contractor's legitimate proprietary interests.

27.403 Data Rights – General.

All contracts that require data to be produced, furnished, acquired, or used in meeting contract performance requirements, must contain terms that delineate the respective rights and obligations of the Government and the contractor regarding the use, reproduction, and disclosure of that data. Data rights clauses do not specify the type, quantity or quality of data that is to be delivered, but only the respective rights of the Government and the contractor regarding the use, disclosure, or reproduction of the data. Accordingly, the contract shall specify the data to be delivered.

27.404 Basic Rights in Data Clause.

This section describes the operation of the clause at 52.227-14, Rights in Data – General, and also the use of the provision at 52.227-15, Representation of Limited Rights Data and Restricted Computer Software.

27.404-1 Unlimited Rights Data

The Government acquires unlimited rights in the following data except for copyrighted works as provided in 27.404-3:

(a) Data first produced in the performance of a contract (except to the extent the data constitute minor modifications to data that are limited rights data or restricted computer software).

(b) Form, fit, and function data delivered under contract.

(c) Data (except as may be included with restricted computer software) that constitute manuals or instructional and training material for installation, operation, or routine maintenance and repair of items, components, or processes delivered or furnished for use under a contract.

(d) All other data delivered under the contract other than limited rights data or restricted computer software (see 27.404-2).

27.404-2 Limited Rights Data and Restricted Computer Software

(a) General. The basic clause at 52.227-14, Rights in Data – General, enables the contractor to protect qualifying limited rights data and restricted computer software by withholding the data from the Government and instead delivering form, fit, and function data.

(b) Alternate definition of limited rights data. For contracts that do not require the development, use, or delivery of items, components, or processes that are intended to be acquired by or for the Government, an agency may adopt the alternate definition of limited rights data set forth in Alternate I to the clause at 52.227-14. The alternate definition does not require that the data pertain to items, components, or processes developed at private expense; but rather that the data were developed at private expense and embody a trade secret or are commercial or financial and confidential or privileged.

(c) Protection of limited rights data specified for delivery.

> (1) The clause at 52.227-14 with its Alternate II enables the Government to require delivery of limited rights data rather than allow the contractor to withhold the data. To obtain delivery, the contract may identify and specify data to be delivered, or the contracting officer may require, by written request during contract performance, the delivery of data that has been withheld or identified to be withheld under paragraph (g)(1) of the clause. In addition, the contract may specifically identify data that are not to be delivered under Alternate II or which, if delivered, will be delivered with limited rights. The limited rights obtained by the Government are set forth in the Limited Rights Notice contained in paragraph (g)(3) of Alternate II. Agencies shall not, without permission of the contractor, use limited rights data for purposes of manufacture or disclose the data outside the Government except as set forth in the Notice. Any disclosure by the Government shall be subject to prohibition against further use and disclosure by the recipient. The following are examples of specific purposes that may

be adopted by an agency in its supplement and added to the Limited Rights Notice of paragraph (g)(3) of Alternate II of the clause:

(i) Use (except for manufacture) by support service contractors.

(ii) Evaluation by nongovernment evaluators.

(iii) Use (except for manufacture) by other contractors participating in the Government's program of which the specific contract is a part.

(iv) Emergency repair or overhaul work.

(v) Release to a foreign government, or its instrumentalities, if required to serve the interests of the U.S. Government, for information or evaluation, or for emergency repair or overhaul work by the foreign government.

(2) The provision at 52.227-15, Representation of Limited Rights Data and Restricted Computer Software, helps the contracting officer to determine whether the clause at 52.227-14 should be used with its Alternate II. This provision requests that an offeror state whether limited rights data are likely to be delivered. Where limited rights data are expected to be delivered, use Alternate II. Where negotiations are based on an unsolicited proposal, the need for Alternate II of the clause at 52.227-14 should be addressed during negotiations or discussions, and if Alternate II was not included initially it may be added by modification, if needed, during contract performance.

(3) If data that would otherwise qualify as limited rights data is delivered as a computer database, the data shall be treated as limited rights data, rather than restricted computer software, for the purposes of paragraph (g) of the clause at 52.227-14.

(d) Protection of restricted computer software specified for delivery.

(1) Alternate III of the clause at 52.227-14, enables the Government to require delivery of restricted computer software rather than allow the contractor to withhold such restricted computer software. To obtain delivery of restricted computer software the contracting officer shall –

(i) Identify and specify the deliverable computer software in the contract; or

(ii) Require by written request during contract performance, the delivery of computer software that has been withheld or identified to be withheld under paragraph (g)(1) of the clause.

(2) In considering whether to use Alternate III, contracting officers should note that, unlike other data, computer software is also an end item in itself. Thus, the contracting officer shall use Alternate III if delivery of restricted computer software is required to meet agency needs.

(3) Unless otherwise agreed (see paragraph (d)(4) of this subsection), the restricted rights obtained by the Government are set forth in the Restricted Rights Notice contained in paragraph (g)(4) (Alternate III). Such restricted computer software will not be used or reproduced by the Government, or disclosed outside the Government, except that the computer software may be –

(i) Used or copied for use with the computers for which it was acquired, including use at any Government installation to which the computers may be transferred;

(ii) Used or copied for use with a backup computer if any computer for which it was acquired is inoperative;

(iii) Reproduced for safekeeping (archives) or backup purposes;

(iv) Modified, adapted, or combined with other computer software, provided that the modified, adapted, or combined portions of the derivative software incorporating any of the delivered, restricted computer software shall be subject to the same restricted rights;

(v) Disclosed to and reproduced for use by support service contractors or their subcontractors, in accordance with paragraphs (3)(i) through (iv) of this section; and

(vi) Used or copied for use with a replacement computer.

(4) The restricted rights set forth in paragraph (d)(3) of this subsection are the minimum rights the Government normally obtains with restricted computer software and will automatically apply when such software is acquired under the Restricted Rights Notice of paragraph (g)(4) of Alternate III of the clause at 52.227-14. However, the contracting officer may specify different rights in the contract, consistent with the purposes and needs for which the software is to be acquired. For example, the contracting officer should consider any networking needs or any requirements for use of the computer software from remote terminals. Also, in addressing such needs, the scope of the restricted rights may be different for the documentation accompanying the computer software than for the programs and databases. Any additions to, or limitations on, the restricted rights set forth in the Restricted Rights Notice of paragraph (g)(4) of Alternate III of the clause at 52.227-14 shall be expressly stated in the contract or in a collateral agreement incorporated in and made part of the contract, and the notice modified accordingly.

(5) The provision at 52.227-15, Representation of Limited Rights Data and Restricted Computer Software, helps the contracting officer determine whether to use the clause at 52.227-14 with its Alternate III. This provision requests that an offeror state whether restricted computer software is likely to be delivered under the contract. In addition, the need for Alternate III should be addressed during negotiations or discussions with an offeror, particularly where negotiations are based on an unsolicited proposal. However, if Alternate III is not used initially, it may be added by modification, if needed, during contract performance.

27.404-3 Copyrighted Works

(a) Data first produced in the performance of a contract.

(1) Generally, the contractor must obtain permission of the contracting officer prior to asserting rights in any copyrighted work containing data first produced in the performance of a contract. However, contractors are normally authorized, without prior approval of the contracting officer, to assert copyright in technical or scientific articles based on or containing such data that is published in academic, technical or professional journals, symposia proceedings and similar works.

(2) The contractor must make a written request for permission to assert its copyright in works containing data first produced under the contract. In its request, the contractor should identify the data involved or furnish copies of the data for which permission is requested, as well as a statement as to the intended publication or dissemination media or other purpose for which the permission is requested. Generally, a contracting officer should grant the contractor's request when copyright protection will enhance the appropriate dissemination or use of the data unless the –

(i) Data consist of a report that represents the official views of the agency or that the agency is required by statute to prepare;

(ii) Data are intended primarily for internal use by the Government;

(iii) Data are of the type that the agency itself distributes to the public under an agency program;

(iv) Government determines that limitation on distribution of the data is in the national interest; or

(v) Government determines that the data should be disseminated without restriction.

(3) Alternate IV of the clause at 52.227-14 provides a substitute paragraph (c)(1) granting permission for contractors to assert copyright in any data first produced in the performance of the contract without the need for any further requests. Except for contracts for management or operation of Government facilities and contracts and subcontracts in support of programs being conducted at those facilities or where international agreements require otherwise, Alternate IV shall be used in all contracts for basic or applied research to be performed solely by colleges and universities. Alternate IV shall not be used in contracts with colleges and universities if a purpose of the contract is for development of computer software for distribution to the public (including use in solicitations) by or on behalf of the Government. In addition, Alternate IV may be used in other contracts if an agency determines that it is not necessary for a contractor to request further permission to assert copyright in data first produced in performance of the contract. The contracting officer may exclude any data, or items or categories of data, from the provisions of Alternate IV by expressly so providing in the contract or by adding a paragraph (d)(4) to the clause, consistent with 27.404-4(b).

(4) Pursuant to paragraph (c)(1) of the clause at 52.227-14, the contractor grants the Government a paid-up nonexclusive, irrevocable, worldwide license to reproduce, prepare derivative works, distribute to the public, perform publicly and display publicly by or on behalf of the Government, for all data (other than computer software) first produced in the performance of a contract. For computer software, the scope of the Government's license includes all of the above rights except the right to distribute to the public. Agencies may also obtain a license of different scope if the contracting officer determines, after consulting with legal counsel, such a license will substantially enhance the dissemination of any data first produced under the contract or if such a license is required to comply with international agreements. If an agency obtains a different license, the contractor shall clearly state the scope of that license in a conspicuous place on the medium on which the data is recorded. For example, if the data is delivered as a

report, the terms of the license shall be stated on the cover, or first page, of the report.

(5) The clause requires the contractor to affix the applicable copyright notices of 17 U.S.C. 401 or 402, and acknowledgment of Government sponsorship, (including the contract number) to data when it asserts copyright in data. Failure to do so could result in such data being treated as unlimited rights data (see 27.404-5(b)).

(b) Data not first produced in the performance of a contract.

(1) Contractors shall not deliver any data that is not first produced under the contract without either –

(i) Acquiring for or granting to the Government a copyright license for the data; or

(ii) Obtaining permission from the contracting officer to do otherwise.

(2) The copyright license the Government acquires for such data will normally be of the same scope as discussed in paragraph (a)(4) of this subsection, and is set forth in paragraph (c)(2) of the clause at 52.227-14. However, agencies may obtain a license of different scope if the agency determines, after consultation with its legal counsel, that such different license will not be inconsistent with the purpose of acquiring the data. If a license of a different scope is acquired, it must be so stated in the contract and clearly set forth in a conspicuous place on the data when delivered to the Government. If the contractor delivers computer software not first produced under the contract, the contractor shall grant the Government the license set forth in paragraph (g)(4) of Alternate III if included in the clause at 52.227-14, or a license agreed to in a collateral agreement made part of the contract.

27.404-4 Contractor's Release, Publication, and Use of Data

(a) In contracts for basic or applied research with universities or colleges, agencies shall not place any restrictions on the conduct of or reporting on the results of unclassified basic or applied research, except as provided in applicable U.S. statutes. However, agencies may restrict the release or disclosure of computer software that is or is intended to be developed to the point of practical application (including for agency distribution under established programs). This is not considered a restriction on the reporting of the results of basic or applied research. Agencies may also preclude a contractor from asserting copyright in any computer software for purposes of established agency distribution programs, or where required to accomplish the purpose for which the software is acquired.

(b) Except for the results of basic or applied research under contracts with universities or colleges, agencies may, to the extent provided in their FAR supplements, place limitations or restrictions on the contractor's exercise of its rights in data first produced in the performance of the contract, including a requirement to assign copyright to the Government or another party. Any of these restrictions shall be expressly included in the contract.

27.404-5 Unauthorized, Omitted, or Incorrect Markings

(a) Unauthorized marking of data.

> (1) The Government has, in accordance with paragraph (e) of the clause at 52.227-14, the right to either return data containing unauthorized markings or to cancel or ignore the markings.
>
> (2) Agencies shall not cancel or ignore markings without making written inquiry of the contractor and affording the contractor at least 60 days to provide a written justification substantiating the propriety of the markings.
>
> > (i) If the contractor fails to respond or fails to provide a written justification substantiating the propriety of the markings within the time afforded, the Government may cancel or ignore the markings.
> >
> > (ii) If the contractor provides a written justification substantiating the propriety of the markings, the contracting officer shall consider the justification.

(A) If the contracting officer determines that the markings are authorized, the contractor will be so notified in writing.

(B) If the contracting officer determines, with concurrence of the head of the contracting activity, that the markings are not authorized, the contractor will be furnished a written determination which becomes the final agency decision regarding the appropriateness of the markings and the markings will be cancelled or ignored and the data will no longer be made subject to disclosure prohibitions, unless the contractor files suit within 90 days in a court of competent jurisdiction. The markings will not be cancelled or ignored until final resolution of the matter, either by the contracting officer's determination becoming the final agency decision or by final disposition of the matter by court decision if suit is filed.

(3) The foregoing procedures may be modified in accordance with agency regulations implementing the Freedom of Information Act (5 U.S.C. 552) if necessary to respond to a request. In addition, the contractor may bring a claim, in accordance with the Disputes clause of the contract, that may arise as the result of the Government's action to remove or ignore any markings on data, unless the action occurs as the result of a final disposition of the matter by a court of competent jurisdiction.

(b) Omitted or incorrect notices.

(1) Data delivered under a contract containing the clause without a limited rights notice or restricted rights notice, and without a copyright notice, will be presumed to have been delivered with unlimited rights, and the Government assumes no liability for the disclosure, use, or reproduction of the data. However, to the extent the data has not been disclosed without restriction outside the Government, the contractor may, within 6 months (or a longer

period approved by the contracting officer for good cause shown), request permission of the contracting officer to have the omitted limited rights or restricted rights notices, as applicable, placed on qualifying data at the contractor's expense. The contracting officer may permit adding appropriate notices if the contractor –

(i) Identifies the data for which a notice is to be added;

(ii) Demonstrates that the omission of the proposed notice was inadvertent;

(iii) Establishes that use of the proposed notice is authorized; and

(iv) Acknowledges that the Government has no liability with respect to any disclosure or use of any such data made prior to the addition of the notice or resulting from the omission of the notice.

(2) The contracting officer may also –

(i) Permit correction, at the contractor's expense, of incorrect notices if the contractor identifies the data on which correction of the notice is to be made, and demonstrates that the correct notice is authorized; or

(ii) Correct any incorrect notices.

27.404-6 Inspection of Data at the Contractor's Facility

Contracting officers may obtain the right to inspect data at the contractor's facility by use of the clause at 52.227-14 with its Alternate V, which adds paragraph (j) to provide that right. Agencies may also adopt Alternate V for general use. The data subject to inspection may be data withheld or withholdable under paragraph (g)(1) of the clause. Inspection may be made by the contracting officer or designee (including nongovernmental personnel under the same conditions as the contracting officer) for the purpose of verifying a contractor's assertion regarding the limited rights or restricted rights status of the data, or for evaluating work performance under the contract. This right may be exercised up to 3 years after acceptance of all items to be delivered under the contract. The contract may specify data items that are not subject to inspection under paragraph (j) of the Alternate. If the contractor demonstrates to the contracting officer that there would be a possible conflict of interest if inspection were made by a particular representative, the contracting officer shall designate an alternate representative.

27.405 Other Data Rights Provisions.

27.405-1 Special Works

(a) The clause at 52.227-17, Rights in Data – Special Works, is for use in contracts (or may be made applicable to portions thereof) that are primarily for the production or compilation of data (other than limited rights data or restricted computer software) for the Government's own use, or when there is a specific need to limit distribution and use of the data or to obtain indemnity for liabilities that may arise out of the content, performance, or disclosure of the data. Examples are contracts for –

(1) The production of audiovisual works, including motion pictures or television recordings with or without accompanying sound, or for the preparation of motion picture scripts, musical compositions, sound tracks, translation, adaptation, and the like;

(2) Histories of the respective agencies, departments, services, or units thereof;

(3) Surveys of Government establishments;

(4) Works pertaining to the instruction or guidance of Government officers and employees in the discharge of their official duties;

(5) The compilation of reports, books, studies, surveys, or similar documents that do not involve research, development, or experimental work;

(6) The collection of data containing personally identifiable information such that the disclosure thereof would violate the right of privacy or publicity of the individual to whom the information relates;

(7) Investigatory reports;

(8) The development, accumulation, or compilation of data (other than that resulting from research, development, or experimental work performed by the contractor), the early release of which could prejudice follow-on acquisition activities or agency regulatory or enforcement activities; or

(9) The development of computer software programs, where the program –

(i) May give a commercial advantage; or

(ii) Is agency mission sensitive, and release could prejudice agency mission, programs, or follow-on acquisitions.

(b) The contract may specify the purposes and conditions (including time limitations) under which the data may be used, released, or reproduced other than for contract performance. Contracts for the production of audiovisual works, sound recordings, etc., may include limitations in connection with talent releases, music licenses, and the like that are consistent with the purposes for which the works are acquired.

(c) Paragraph (c)(1)(ii) of the clause, which enables the Government to obtain assignment of copyright in any data first produced in the performance of the contract, may be deleted if the contracting officer determines that such assignment is not needed to further the objectives of the contract.

(d) Paragraph (e) of the clause, which requires the contractor to indemnify the Government against any liability incurred as the result of any violation of trade secrets, copyrights, right of privacy or publicity, or any libelous or other unlawful matter arising out of or contained in any production or compilation of data that are subject to the clause, may be deleted or limited in scope where the contracting officer determines that, because of the nature of the particular data involved, such liability will not arise.

(e) When the audiovisual or other special works are produced to accomplish a public purpose other than acquisition for the Government's own use (such as for production and distribution to the public of the works by other than a Federal agency) agencies are authorized to modify the clause for use in contracts, with rights in data provisions that meet agency mission needs yet protect free speech and freedom of expression, as well as the artistic license of the creator of the work.

27.405-2 Existing Works

The clause at 52.227-18, Rights in Data – Existing Works, is for use in contracts exclusively for the acquisition (without modification) of existing works such as, motion pictures, television recordings, and other audiovisual works; sound recordings; musical, dramatic, and literary works; pantomimes and choreographic works; pictorial, graphic, and sculptural works; and works of a similar nature. The contract may set forth limitations consistent with the purposes for which the works covered by the contract are being acquired. Examples of these limitations are means of exhibition or transmission, time, type of audience, and geographical location. However, if the contract requires that works of the type indicated in this paragraph are to be modified through editing, translation, or addition of subject matter, etc. (rather than purchased in existing form), then see 27.405-1.

27.405-3 Commercial Computer Software

(a) When contracting other than from GSA's Multiple Award Schedule contracts for the acquisition of commercial computer software, no specific contract clause prescribed in this subpart need be used, but the contract shall specifically address the Government's rights to use, disclose, modify, distribute, and reproduce the software. Section 12.212 sets forth the guidance for the acquisition of commercial computer software and states that commercial computer software or commercial computer software documentation shall be acquired under licenses customarily provided to the public to the extent the license is consistent with Federal law and otherwise satisfies the Government's needs. The clause at 52.227-19, Commercial Computer Software License, may be used when there is any confusion as to whether the Government's needs are satisfied or whether a customary commercial license is consistent with Federal law. Additional or lesser rights may be negotiated using the guidance concerning restricted rights as set forth in 27.404-2(d), or the clause at 52.227-19. If greater rights than the minimum rights identified in the clause at 52.227-19 are needed, or lesser rights are to be acquired, they shall be negotiated and set forth in the contract. This includes any additions to, or limitations on, the rights set forth in paragraph (b) of the clause at 52.227-19 when used. Examples of greater rights may be those necessary for networking purposes or use of the software from remote terminals communicating with a host computer where the software is located. If the computer software is to be acquired with unlimited rights, the contract shall also so state. In addition, the contract shall adequately describe the computer programs and/or databases, the media on which it is recorded, and all the necessary documentation.

(b) If the contract incorporates, makes reference to, or uses a vendor's standard commercial lease, license, or purchase agreement, the contracting officer shall ensure that the agreement is consistent with paragraph (a)(1) of this subsection. The contracting officer should exercise caution in accepting a vendor's terms and conditions, since they may be directed to commercial sales and may not be appropriate for Government contracts. Any inconsistencies in a vendor's standard commercial agreement shall be addressed in the contract and the contract terms shall take precedence over the vendor's standard commercial agreement. If the clause at 52.227-19 is used, inconsistencies in the vendor's standard commercial agreement regarding the Government's right to use, reproduce or disclose the computer software are reconciled by that clause.

(c) If a prime contractor under a contract containing the clause at 52.227-14, Rights in Data – General, with paragraph (g)(4) (Alternate III) in the clause, acquires restricted computer software from a subcontractor (at any tier) as a separate acquisition for delivery to or for use on behalf of the Government, the contracting officer may approve any additions to, or limitations on the restricted rights in the Restricted Rights Notice of paragraph (g)(4) in a collateral agreement incorporated in and made part of the contract.

27.405-4 Other Existing Data

(a) Except for existing works pursuant to 27.405-2 or commercial computer software pursuant to 27.405-3, no clause contained in this subpart is required to be included in –

(1) Contracts solely for the acquisition of books, periodicals, and other printed items in the exact form in which these items are to be obtained unless reproduction rights are to be acquired; or

(2) Other contracts that require only existing data (other than limited rights data) to be delivered and the data are available without disclosure prohibitions, unless reproduction rights to the data are to be obtained.

(b) If the reproduction rights to the data are to be obtained in any contract of the type described in paragraph (b)(1) (i) or (ii) of this section, the rights shall be specifically set forth in the contract. No clause contained in this subpart is required to be included in contracts substantially for on-line data base services in the same form as they are normally available to the general public.

27.406 Acquisition of Data.

27.406-1 General

(a) It is the Government's practice to determine, to the extent feasible, its data requirements in time for inclusion in solicitations. The data requirements may be subject to revision during contract negotiations. Since the preparation, reformatting, maintenance and updating, cataloging, and storage of data represents an expense to both the Government and the contractor, efforts should be made to keep the contract data requirements to a minimum, consistent with the purposes of the contract.

(b) The contracting officer shall specify in the contract all known data requirements, including the time and place for delivery and any limitations and restrictions to be imposed on the contractor in the handling of the data. Further, and to the extent feasible, in major system acquisitions, the contracting officer shall set out data requirements as separate contract line items. In establishing the contract data requirements and in specifying data items to be delivered by a contractor, agencies may, consistent with paragraph (a) of this subsection, develop their own contract schedule provisions. Agency procedures may, among other things, provide for listing, specifying, identifying source, assuring delivery, and handling any data required to be delivered, first produced, or specifically used in the performance of the contract.

(c) Data delivery requirements should normally not require that a contractor provide the Government, as a condition of the procurement, unlimited rights in data that qualify as limited rights data or restricted computer software. Rather, form, fit, and function data may be furnished with unlimited rights instead of the qualifying data, or the qualifying data may be furnished with limited rights or restricted rights if needed (see 27.404-2(c) and (d)). If greater rights are needed, they should be clearly set forth in the solicitation and the contractor fairly compensated for the greater rights.

27.406-2 Additional Data Requirements.

(a) In some contracting situations, such as experimental, developmental, research, or demonstration contracts, it may not be feasible to ascertain all the data requirements at contract award. The clause at 52.227-16, Additional Data Requirements, may be used to enable the subsequent ordering by the contracting officer of additional data first produced or specifically used in the performance of these contracts as the actual requirements become known. The clause shall normally be used in solicitations and contracts involving experimental, developmental, research or demonstration work (other than basic or applied research to be performed under a contract solely by a university or college when the contract amount will be $500,000 or less) unless all the requirements for data are believed to be known at the time of contracting and specified in the contract. If the contract is for basic or applied research to be performed by a university or college, and the contracting officer believes the contract effort will in the future exceed $500,000, even though the initial award does not, the contracting officer may include the clause in the initial award.

(b) Data may be ordered under the clause at 52.227-16 at any time during contract performance or within a period of 3 years after acceptance of all items to be delivered under the contract. The contractor is to be compensated for converting the data into the prescribed form, for reproduction, and for delivery. In order to minimize storage costs for the retention of data, the contracting officer may relieve the contractor of the retention requirements for specified data items at any time during the retention period required by the clause. The contracting officer may permit the contractor to identify and specify in the contract data not to be ordered for delivery under the clause if the data is not necessary to meet the Government's requirements for data. Also, the contracting officer may alter the clause by deleting the term "or specifically used" in paragraph (a) of the clause if delivery of the data is not necessary to meet the Government's requirements for data. Any data ordered under this clause will be subject to the clause at 52.227-14, Rights in Data – General, (or other equivalent clause setting forth the respective rights of the Government and the contractor) in the contract. Data authorized to be withheld under such clause will not be required to be delivered under the clause at 52.227-16, except as provided in Alternate II or Alternate III, if included (see 27.404-2(c) and (d)).

(c) Absent an established program for dissemination of computer software, agencies should not order additional computer software under the clause at 52.227-16, for the sole purpose of disseminating or marketing the software to the public. In ordering software for internal purposes, the contracting officer shall consider, consistent with the Government's needs, not ordering particular source codes, algorithms, processes, formulas, or flow charts of the software if the contractor shows that this aids its efforts to disseminate or market the software.

27.406-3 Major System Acquisition

(a) The clause at 52.227-21, Technical Data Declaration, Revision, and Withholding of Payment – Major Systems, implements 41 U.S.C. 415a(d). When using the clause at 52.227-21, the section of the contract specifying data delivery requirements (see 27.406-1(b)) shall expressly identify those line items of technical data to which the clause applies. Upon delivery of the technical data, the contracting officer shall review the technical data and the contractor's declaration relating to it to assure that the data are complete, accurate, and comply with contract requirements. If the data are not complete, accurate, or compliant, the contracting officer should request the contractor to correct the deficiencies, and may withhold payment. Final payment shall not be made under the contract until it has been determined that the delivery requirements of those line items of data to which the clause applies have been satisfactorily met.

(b) In a contract for, or in support of, a major system awarded by a civilian agency other than NASA or the U.S. Coast Guard, the following applies:

(1) The contracting officer shall require the delivery of any technical data relating to the major system or supplies for the major system, that are to be developed exclusively with Federal funds if the delivery of the technical data is needed to ensure the competitive acquisition of supplies or services that will be required in substantial quantities in the future. The clause at 52.227-22, Major System – Minimum Rights, is used in addition to the clause at 52.227-14, Rights in Data – General, and other required clauses, to ensure that the Government acquires at least those rights required by Pub. L. 98-577 in technical data developed exclusively with Federal funds.

(2) Technical data, relating to a major system or supplies for a major system, procured or to be procured by the Government and also relating to the design, development, or manufacture of products or processes offered or to be offered for sale to the public (except for such data as may be necessary for the Government to operate or maintain the product, or use the process if obtained by the Government as an element of performance under the contract), shall not be required to be provided to the Government from persons who have developed such products or processes as a condition for the procurement of such products or processes by the Government.

27.407 Rights to Technical Data in Successful Proposals.

The clause at 52.227-23, Rights to Proposal Data (Technical), allows the Government to acquire unlimited rights to technical data in successful proposals. Pursuant to the clause, the prospective contractor is afforded the opportunity to specifically identify pages containing technical data to be excluded from the grant of unlimited rights. This exclusion is not dispositive of the protective status of the data, but any excluded technical data, as well as any commercial and financial information contained in the proposal, will remain subject to the policies in Subpart 15.2 or 15.6 (or agency supplements) relating to proposal information (e.g., will be used for evaluation purposes only). If there is a need to have access to any of the excluded technical data during contract performance, consideration should be given to acquiring the data with limited rights, if they so qualify, in accordance with 27.404-2(c).

27.408 Cosponsored Research and Development Activities.

(a) In contracts involving cosponsored research and development that require the contractor to make substantial contributions of funds or resources (e.g., by cost-sharing or by repayment of nonrecurring costs), and the contractor's and the Government's respective contributions to any item, component, process, or computer software, developed or produced under the contract are not readily segregable, the contracting officer may limit the acquisition of, or acquire less than unlimited rights to, any data developed and delivered under the contract. Agencies may regulate the use of this authority in their supplements. Lesser rights shall, at a minimum, assure use of the data for agreed-to Governmental purposes (including reprocurement rights as appropriate), and address any disclosure limitations or restrictions to be imposed on the data. Also, consideration may be given to requiring the contractor to directly license others if needed to carry out the objectives of the contract. Since the purpose of the cosponsored research and development, the legitimate proprietary interests of the contractor, the needs of the Government, and the respective contributions of both parties may vary, no specific clauses are prescribed, but a clause providing less than unlimited rights in the Government for data developed and delivered under the contract (such as license rights) may be tailored to the circumstances consistent with the foregoing and the policy set forth in 27.402. As a guide, a clause may be appropriate when the contractor contributes money or resources, or agrees to make repayment of nonrecurring costs, of a value of approximately 50 percent of the total cost of the contract (i.e., Government, contractor, and/or third party paid costs), and the respective contributions are not readily segregable for any work element to be performed under the contract. A clause may be used for all or for only specifically identified tasks or work elements under the contract. In the latter instance, its use will be in addition to whatever other data rights clause is prescribed under this subpart, with the contract specifically identifying which clause is to apply to which tasks or work elements. Further, this type of clause may not be appropriate where the purpose of the contract is to produce data for dissemination to the public, or to develop or demonstrate technologies that will be available, in any event, to the public for its direct use.

(b) Where the contractor's contributions are readily segregable (by performance requirements and the funding for the contract) and so identified in the contract, any resulting data may be treated under this clause as limited rights data or restricted computer software in accordance with 27.404-2(c) or (d), as applicable; or if this treatment is inconsistent with the purpose of the contract, rights to the data may, if so negotiated and stated in the contract, be treated in a manner consistent with paragraph (a) of this section.

27.409 Solicitation Provisions and Contract Clauses.

(a) Generally, a contract should contain only one data rights clause. However, where more than one is needed, the contract should distinguish the portion of contract performance to which each pertains.

(b)

(1) Insert the clause at 52.227-14, Rights in Data – General, in solicitations and contracts if it is contemplated that data will be produced, furnished, or acquired under the contract, unless the contract is –

(i) For the production of special works of the type set forth in 27.405-1, although in these cases insert the clause at 52.227-14, Rights in Data – General, and make it applicable to data other than special works, as appropriate (see paragraph (e) of this section);

(ii) For the acquisition of existing data, commercial computer software, or other existing data, as described in 27.405-2 through 27.405-4 (see paragraphs (f) and (g) of this section);

(iii) A small business innovation research contract (see paragraph (h) of this section);

(iv) To be performed outside the United States (see paragraph (i)(1) of this section);

(v) For architect-engineer services or construction work (see paragraph (i)(2) of this section);

(vi) For the management, operation, design, or construction of a Government-owned facility to perform research, development, or production work (see paragraph (i)(3) of this section); or

(vii) A contract involving cosponsored research and development in which a clause providing for less than unlimited right has been authorized (see 27.408).

(2) If an agency determines, in accordance with 27.404-2(b), to adopt the alternate definition of "Limited Rights Data" in paragraph (a) of the clause, use the clause with its Alternate I.

(3) If a contracting officer determines, in accordance with 27.404-2(c) that it is necessary to obtain limited rights data, use the clause with its Alternate II. The contracting officer shall complete paragraph (g)(3) to include the purposes, if any, for which limited rights data are to be disclosed outside the Government.

(4) In accordance with 27.404-2(d), if a contracting officer determines it is necessary to obtain restricted computer software, use the clause with its Alternate III. Any greater or lesser rights regarding the use, reproduction, or disclosure of restricted computer software than those set forth in the Restricted Rights Notice of paragraph (g)(4) of the clause shall be specified in the contract and the notice modified accordingly.

(5) Use the clause with its Alternate IV in contracts for basic or applied research (other than those for the management or operation of Government facilities, and contracts and subcontracts in support of programs being conducted at those facilities or where international agreements require otherwise) to be performed solely by universities and colleges. The clause may be used with its

Alternate IV in other contracts if in accordance with 27.404-3(a), an agency determines to grant permission for the contractor to assert claim to copyright subsisting in all data first produced without further request being made by the contractor. When Alternate IV is used, the contract may exclude items or categories of data from the permission granted, either by express provisions in the contract or by the addition of a paragraph (d)(4) to the clause (see 27.404-4).

(6) In accordance with 27.404-6, if the Government needs the right to inspect certain data at a contractor's facility, use the clause with its Alternate V.

(c) In accordance with 27.404-2(c)(2) and 27.404-2(d)(5), if the contracting officer desires to have an offeror state in response to a solicitation whether limited rights data or restricted computer software are likely to be used in meeting the data delivery requirements set forth in the solicitation, insert the provision at 52.227-15, Representation of Limited Rights Data and Restricted Computer Software, in any solicitation containing the clause at 52.227-14, Rights in Data – General. The contractor's response may provide an aid in determining whether the clause should be used with Alternate II and/or Alternate III.

(d) Insert the clause at 52.227-16, Additional Data Requirements, in solicitations and contracts involving experimental, developmental, research, or demonstration work (other than basic or applied research to be performed solely by a university or college where the contract amount will be $500,000 or less) unless all the requirements for data are believed to be known at the time of contracting and specified in the contract (see 27.406-2). This clause may also be used in other contracts when considered appropriate. For example, if the contract is for basic or applied research to be performed by a university or college, and the contracting officer believes the contract effort will in the future exceed $500,000, even though the initial award does not, the contracting officer may include the clause in the initial award.

(e) In accordance with 27.405-1, insert the clause at 52.227-17, Rights in Data – Special Works, in solicitations and contracts primarily for the production or compilation of data (other than limited rights data or restricted computer software) for the Government's internal use, or when there is a specific need to limit distribution and use of the data or to obtain indemnity for liabilities that may arise out of the content, performance, or disclosure of the data. Examples of such contracts are set forth in 27.405-1.

(1) Insert the clause if existing works are to be modified, as by editing, translation, addition of subject matter, etc.

(2) The contract may specify the purposes and conditions (including time limitations) under which the data may be used, released, or reproduced by the contractor for other than contract performance.

(3) Contracts for the production of audiovisual works, sound recordings, etc. may include limitations in connection with talent releases, music licenses, and the like that are consistent with the purposes for which the data is acquired.

(4) The clause may be modified in accordance with paragraphs (c) through (e) of 27.405-1.

(f) Insert the clause at 52.227-18, Rights in Data – Existing Works, in solicitations and contracts exclusively for the acquisition, without modification, of existing audiovisual and similar works of the type set forth in 27.405-2. The contract may set forth limitations consistent with the purposes for which the work is being acquired. While no specific clause of this subpart is required to be included in contracts solely for the acquisition, without disclosure prohibitions, of books, publications, and similar items in the exact form in which the items exist prior to the request for purchase (i.e., the off-the-shelf purchase of such items), or in other contracts where only existing data available without disclosure prohibitions is to be furnished, if reproduction rights are to be acquired, the contract shall include terms addressing such rights. (See 27.405-4.)

(g) In accordance with 27.405-3, when contracting (other than from GSA's Multiple Award Schedule contracts) for the acquisition of commercial computer software, the contracting officer may insert the clause at 52.227-19, Commercial Computer Software License, in the solicitation and contract. In any event, the contracting officer shall assure that the contract contains terms to obtain sufficient rights for the Government to fulfill the need for which the software is being acquired and is otherwise consistent with 27.405-3.

(h) If the contract is a Small Business Innovation Research (SBIR) contract, insert the clause at 52.227-20, Rights in Data – SBIR Program in all Phase I, Phase II, and Phase III contracts awarded under the Small Business Innovation Research Program established pursuant to 15 U.S.C. 638. The SBIR protection period may be extended in accordance with the Small Business Administration's "Small Business Innovation Research Program Policy Directive" (September 24, 2002).

(i) Agencies may prescribe in their procedures, as appropriate, a clause consistent with the policy of 27.402 in contracts –

> (1) To be performed outside the United States;
>
> (2) For architect-engineer services and construction work (e.g., the clause at 52.227-17, Rights in Data – Special Works); or
>
> (3) For management, operation, design, or construction of Government-owned research, development, or production facilities, and in contracts and subcontracts in support of programs being conducted at such facilities.

(j) In accordance with 27.406-3(a), insert the clause at 52.227-21, Technical Data Declaration, Revision, and Withholding of Payment – Major Systems, in contracts for major systems acquisitions or for support of major systems acquisitions. This requirement includes contracts for detailed design, development, or production of a major system and contracts for any individual part, component, subassembly, assembly, or subsystem integral to the major system, and other property that may be replaced during the service life of the system, including spare parts. When used, this clause requires that the technical data to which it applies be specified in the contract (see 27.406-3(a)).

(k) In accordance with 24.706(b), in the case of civilian agencies other than NASA and the U.S. Coast Guard, insert the clause at 52.227-22, Major

System – Minimum Rights, in contracts for major systems or contracts in support of major systems.

(l) In accordance with 27.407, if a contracting officer desires to acquire unlimited rights in technical data contained in a successful proposal upon which a contract award is based, insert the clause at 52.227-23, Rights to Proposal Data (Technical). Rights to technical data in a proposal are not acquired by mere incorporation by reference of the proposal in the contract, and if a proposal is incorporated by reference, the contracting officer shall follow 27.404 to assure that the rights are appropriately addressed.

Subpart 27.5 – FOREIGN LICENSE AND TECHNICAL ASSISTANT AGREEMENTS

27.501 General.

Agencies shall provide necessary policy and procedures regarding foreign technical assistance agreements and license agreements involving intellectual property, including avoiding unnecessary royalty charges.

Courtesy of William C. Bergmann, Baker Hostetler LLP

APPENDIX E

FEDERAL ACQUISITION REGULATION, PART 52

PART 52 – SOLICITATION PROVISIONS AND CONTRACT CLAUSES

52.212-4 Contract Terms and Conditions – Commercial Items

As prescribed in 12.301(b)(3), insert the following clause:

CONTRACT TERMS AND CONDITIONS – COMMERCIAL ITEMS (OCT 2008)

(a) Inspection/Acceptance. The Contractor shall only tender for acceptance those items that conform to the requirements of this contract. The Government reserves the right to inspect or test any supplies or services that have been tendered for acceptance. The Government may require repair or replacement of nonconforming supplies or reperformance of nonconforming services at no increase in contract price. If repair/replacement or reperformance will not correct the defects or is not possible, the Government may seek an equitable price reduction or adequate consideration for acceptance of nonconforming supplies or services. The Government must exercise its post-acceptance rights –

(1) Within a reasonable time after the defect was discovered or should have been discovered; and

(2) Before any substantial change occurs in the condition of the item, unless the change is due to the defect in the item.

(b) Assignment. The Contractor or its assignee may assign its rights to receive payment due as a result of performance of this contract to a bank, trust company, or other financing institution, including any Federal lending agency in accordance with the Assignment of Claims Act (31 U.S.C. 3727). However, when a third party makes payment (e.g., use of the Governmentwide commercial purchase card), the Contractor may not assign its rights to receive payment under this contract.

(c) Changes. Changes in the terms and conditions of this contract may be made only by written agreement of the parties.

(d) Disputes. This contract is subject to the Contract Disputes Act of 1978, as amended (41 U.S.C. 601-613). Failure of the parties to this contract to reach agreement on any request for equitable adjustment, claim, appeal or action arising under or relating to this contract shall be a dispute to be resolved in accordance with the clause at FAR 52.233-1, Disputes, which is incorporated herein by reference. The Contractor shall proceed diligently with performance of this contract, pending final resolution of any dispute arising under the contract.

(e) Definitions. The clause at FAR 52.202-1, Definitions, is incorporated herein by reference.

(f) Excusable delays. The Contractor shall be liable for default unless nonperformance is caused by an occurrence beyond the reasonable control of the Contractor and without its fault or negligence such as, acts of God or the public enemy, acts of the Government in either its sovereign or contractual capacity, fires, floods, epidemics, quarantine restrictions, strikes, unusually severe weather, and delays of common carriers. The Contractor shall notify the Contracting Officer in writing as soon as it is reasonably possible after the commencement of any excusable delay, setting forth the full particulars in connection therewith, shall remedy such occurrence with all reasonable dispatch, and shall promptly give written notice to the Contracting Officer of the cessation of such occurrence.

(g) Invoice.

(1) The Contractor shall submit an original invoice and three copies (or electronic invoice, if authorized) to the address designated in the contract to receive invoices. An invoice must include –

(i) Name and address of the Contractor;

(ii) Invoice date and number;

(iii) Contract number, contract line item number and, if applicable, the order number;

(iv) Description, quantity, unit of measure, unit price and extended price of the items delivered;

(v) Shipping number and date of shipment, including the bill of lading number and weight of shipment if shipped on Government bill of lading;

(vi) Terms of any discount for prompt payment offered;

(vii) Name and address of official to whom payment is to be sent;

(viii) Name, title, and phone number of person to notify in event of defective invoice; and

(ix) Taxpayer Identification Number (TIN). The Contractor shall include its TIN on the invoice only if required elsewhere in this contract.

(x) Electronic funds transfer (EFT) banking information.

> (A) The Contractor shall include EFT banking information on the invoice only if required elsewhere in this contract.
>
> (B) If EFT banking information is not required to be on the invoice, in order for the invoice to be a proper invoice, the Contractor shall have submitted correct EFT banking information in accordance with the applicable solicitation provision, contract clause (e.g., 52.232-33, Payment by Electronic Funds Transfer – Central Contractor Registration, or 52.232-34, Payment by Electronic Funds Transfer – Other Than Central Contractor Registration), or applicable agency procedures.
>
> (C) EFT banking information is not required if the Government waived the requirement to pay by EFT.

(2) Invoices will be handled in accordance with the Prompt Payment Act (31 U.S.C. 3903) and Office of Management and Budget (OMB) prompt payment regulations at 5 CFR Part 1315.

(h) Patent indemnity. The Contractor shall indemnify the Government and its officers, employees and agents against liability, including costs, for actual or alleged direct or contributory infringement of, or inducement to infringe, any United States or foreign patent, trademark or copyright, arising out of the performance of this contract, provided the Contractor is reasonably notified of such claims and proceedings.

(i) Payment –

(1) Items accepted. Payment shall be made for items accepted by the Government that have been delivered to the delivery destinations set forth in this contract.

(2) Prompt payment. The Government will make payment in accordance with the Prompt Payment Act (31 U.S.C. 3903) and prompt payment regulations at 5 CFR Part 1315.

(3) Electronic Funds Transfer (EFT). If the Government makes payment by EFT, see 52.212-5(b) for the appropriate EFT clause.

(4) Discount. In connection with any discount offered for early payment, time shall be computed from the date of the invoice. For the purpose of computing the discount earned, payment shall be considered to have been made on the date which appears on the payment check or the specified payment date if an electronic funds transfer payment is made.

(5) Overpayments. If the Contractor becomes aware of a duplicate contract financing or invoice payment or that the Government has otherwise overpaid on a contract financing or invoice payment, the Contractor shall –

(i) Remit the overpayment amount to the payment office cited in the contract along with a description of the overpayment including the –

(A) Circumstances of the overpayment (e.g., duplicate payment, erroneous payment, liquidation errors, date(s) of overpayment);

(B) Affected contract number and delivery order number, if applicable;

(C) Affected contract line item or subline item, if applicable; and

(D) Contractor point of contact.

(ii) Provide a copy of the remittance and supporting documentation to the Contracting Officer.

(6) Interest.

(i) All amounts that become payable by the Contractor to the Government under this contract shall bear simple interest from the date due until paid unless paid within 30 days of becoming due. The interest rate shall be the interest rate established by the Secretary of the Treasury as provided in Section 611 of the Contract Disputes Act of 1978 (Public Law 95-563), which is applicable to the period in which the amount becomes due, as provided in (i)(6)(v) of this clause, and then at the rate applicable for each six-month period as fixed by the Secretary until the amount is paid.

(ii) The Government may issue a demand for payment to the Contractor upon finding a debt is due under the contract.

(iii) Final decisions. The Contracting Officer will issue a final decision as required by 33.211 if –

(A) The Contracting Officer and the Contractor are unable to reach agreement on the existence or amount of a debt within 30 days;

(B) The Contractor fails to liquidate a debt previously demanded by the Contracting Officer within the timeline specified in the demand for payment unless the amounts were not repaid because the Contractor has requested an installment payment agreement; or

(C) The Contractor requests a deferment of collection on a debt previously demanded by the Contracting Officer (see 32.607-2).

(iv) If a demand for payment was previously issued for the debt, the demand for payment included in the final decision shall identify the same due date as the original demand for payment.

(v) Amounts shall be due at the earliest of the following dates:

(A) The date fixed under this contract.

(B) The date of the first written demand for payment, including any demand for payment resulting from a default termination.

(vi) The interest charge shall be computed for the actual number of calendar days involved beginning on the due date and ending on –

(A) The date on which the designated office receives payment from the Contractor;

(B) The date of issuance of a Government check to the Contractor from which an amount otherwise payable has been withheld as a credit against the contract debt; or

(C) The date on which an amount withheld and applied to the contract debt would otherwise have become payable to the Contractor.

(vii) The interest charge made under this clause may be reduced under the procedures prescribed in 32.608-2 of the Federal Acquisition Regulation in effect on the date of this contract.

(j) Risk of loss. Unless the contract specifically provides otherwise, risk of loss or damage to the supplies provided under this contract shall remain with the Contractor until, and shall pass to the Government upon:

(1) Delivery of the supplies to a carrier, if transportation is f.o.b. origin; or

(2) Delivery of the supplies to the Government at the destination specified in the contract, if transportation is f.o.b. destination.

(k) Taxes. The contract price includes all applicable Federal, State, and local taxes and duties.

(l) Termination for the Government's convenience. The Government reserves the right to terminate this contract, or any part hereof, for its sole convenience. In the event of such termination, the Contractor shall immediately stop all work hereunder and shall immediately cause any and all of its suppliers and subcontractors to cease work. Subject to the terms of this contract, the Contractor shall be paid a percentage of the contract price reflecting the percentage of the work performed prior to the notice of termination, plus reasonable charges the Contractor can demonstrate to the satisfaction of the Government using its standard record keeping system, have resulted from the termination. The Contractor shall not be required to comply with the cost accounting standards or contract cost principles for this purpose. This paragraph does not give the Government any right to audit the Contractor's records. The Contractor shall not be paid for any work performed or costs incurred which reasonably could have been avoided.

(m) Termination for cause. The Government may terminate this contract, or any part hereof, for cause in the event of any default by the Contractor, or if the Contractor fails to comply with any contract terms and conditions, or fails to provide the Government, upon request, with adequate assurances of future performance. In the event of termination for cause, the

Government shall not be liable to the Contractor for any amount for supplies or services not accepted, and the Contractor shall be liable to the Government for any and all rights and remedies provided by law. If it is determined that the Government improperly terminated this contract for default, such termination shall be deemed a termination for convenience.

(n) Title. Unless specified elsewhere in this contract, title to items furnished under this contract shall pass to the Government upon acceptance, regardless of when or where the Government takes physical possession.

(o) Warranty. The Contractor warrants and implies that the items delivered hereunder are merchantable and fit for use for the particular purpose described in this contract.

(p) Limitation of liability. Except as otherwise provided by an express warranty, the Contractor will not be liable to the Government for consequential damages resulting from any defect or deficiencies in accepted items.

(q) Other compliances. The Contractor shall comply with all applicable Federal, State and local laws, executive orders, rules and regulations applicable to its performance under this contract.

(r) Compliance with laws unique to Government contracts. The Contractor agrees to comply with 31 U.S.C. 1352 relating to limitations on the use of appropriated funds to influence certain Federal contracts; 18 U.S.C. 431 relating to officials not to benefit; 40 U.S.C. 3701, et seq., Contract Work Hours and Safety Standards Act; 41 U.S.C. 51-58, Anti-Kickback Act of 1986; 41 U.S.C. 265 and 10 U.S.C. 2409 relating to whistleblower protections; 49 U.S.C. 40118, Fly American; and 41 U.S.C. 423 relating to procurement integrity.

(s) Order of precedence. Any inconsistencies in this solicitation or contract shall be resolved by giving precedence in the following order:

(1) The schedule of supplies/services.

(2) The Assignments, Disputes, Payments, Invoice, Other Compliances, and Compliance with Laws Unique to Government Contracts paragraphs of this clause.

(3) The clause at 52.212-5.

(4) Addenda to this solicitation or contract, including any license agreements for computer software.

(5) Solicitation provisions if this is a solicitation.

(6) Other paragraphs of this clause.

(7) The Standard Form 1449.

(8) Other documents, exhibits, and attachments.

(9) The specification.

(t) Central Contractor Registration (CCR).

(1) Unless exempted by an addendum to this contract, the Contractor is responsible during performance and through final payment of any contract for the accuracy and completeness of the data within the CCR database, and for any liability resulting from the Government's reliance on inaccurate or incomplete data. To remain registered in the CCR database after the initial registration, the Contractor is required to review and update on an annual basis from the date of initial registration or subsequent updates its information in the CCR database to ensure it is current, accurate and complete. Updating information in the CCR does not alter the terms and conditions of this contract and is not a substitute for a properly executed contractual document.

(2)

(i) If a Contractor has legally changed its business name, "doing business as" name, or division name (whichever is shown on the contract), or has transferred the assets used in performing the contract, but has not completed the necessary requirements regarding novation and change-of-name agreements in FAR Subpart 42.12, the Contractor shall provide the responsible Contracting Officer a minimum of one business day's written notification of its intention to (A) change the name in the CCR database; (B) comply with the requirements of Subpart 42.12; and (C) agree in writing to the timeline and procedures specified by the responsible Contracting Officer. The Contractor must provide with the notification sufficient documentation to support the legally changed name.

(ii) If the Contractor fails to comply with the requirements of paragraph (t)(2)(i) of this clause, or fails to perform the agreement at paragraph (t)(2)(i)(C) of this clause, and, in the absence of a properly executed novation or change-of-name agreement, the CCR information that shows the Contractor to be other than the Contractor indicated in the contract will be considered to be incorrect information within the meaning of the "Suspension of Payment" paragraph of the electronic funds transfer (EFT) clause of this contract.

(3) The Contractor shall not change the name or address for EFT payments or manual payments, as appropriate, in the CCR record to reflect an assignee for the purpose of assignment of claims (see Subpart 32.8, Assignment of Claims). Assignees shall be separately registered in the CCR database. Information provided to the Contractor's CCR record that indicates payments, including those made by EFT, to an ultimate recipient other than that Contractor will be considered to be incorrect information within the meaning of the "Suspension of payment" paragraph of the EFT clause of this contract.

(4) Offerors and Contractors may obtain information on registration and annual confirmation requirements via the internet at http://www.ccr.gov or by calling 1-888-227-2423 or 269-961-5757.

(End of clause)

Alternate I (Oct 2008). When a time-and-materials or labor-hour contract is contemplated, substitute the following paragraphs (a), (e), (i) and (l) for those in the basic clause.

(a) Inspection/Acceptance.

(1) The Government has the right to inspect and test all materials furnished and services performed under this contract, to the extent practicable at all places and times, including the period of performance, and in any event before acceptance. The Government may also inspect the plant or plants of the Contractor or any subcontractor engaged in contract performance. The Government will perform inspections and tests in a manner that will not unduly delay the work.

(2) If the Government performs inspection or tests on the premises of the Contractor or a subcontractor, the Contractor shall furnish and shall require subcontractors to furnish all reasonable facilities and assistance for the safe and convenient performance of these duties.

(3) Unless otherwise specified in the contract, the Government will accept or reject services and materials at the place of delivery as promptly as practicable after delivery, and they will be presumed accepted 60 days after the date of delivery, unless accepted earlier.

(4) At any time during contract performance, but not later than 6 months (or such other time as may be specified in the contract) after acceptance of the services or materials last delivered under this contract, the Government may require the Contractor to replace or correct services or materials that at time of delivery failed to meet contract requirements. Except as otherwise specified in paragraph (a)(6) of this clause, the cost of replacement or correction shall be determined under paragraph (i) of this clause, but the "hourly rate" for labor hours incurred in the replacement or correction shall be reduced to exclude that portion of the rate attributable to profit. Unless otherwise specified below, the portion of the "hourly rate" attributable to profit shall be 10 percent. The Contractor shall not tender for acceptance materials and services required to be replaced or corrected without disclosing the former requirement for replacement or correction, and, when required, shall disclose the corrective action taken. [Insert portion of labor rate attributable to profit.]

(5)

(i) If the Contractor fails to proceed with reasonable promptness to perform required replacement or correction, and if the replacement or correction can be performed within the ceiling price (or the ceiling price as increased by the Government), the Government may –

(A) By contract or otherwise, perform the replacement or correction, charge to the Contractor any increased cost, or deduct such increased cost from any amounts paid or due under this contract; or

(B) Terminate this contract for cause.

(ii) Failure to agree to the amount of increased cost to be charged to the Contractor shall be a dispute under the Disputes clause of the contract.

(6) Notwithstanding paragraphs (a)(4) and (5) above, the Government may at any time require the Contractor to remedy by correction or replacement, without cost to the Government, any failure by the Contractor to comply with the requirements of this contract, if the failure is due to –

(i) Fraud, lack of good faith, or willful misconduct on the part of the Contractor's managerial personnel; or

(ii) The conduct of one or more of the Contractor's employees selected or retained by the Contractor after any of the Contractor's managerial personnel has reasonable grounds to believe that the employee is habitually careless or unqualified.

(7) This clause applies in the same manner and to the same extent to corrected or replacement materials or services as to materials and services originally delivered under this contract.

(8) The Contractor has no obligation or liability under this contract to correct or replace materials and services that at time of delivery do not meet contract requirements, except as provided in this clause or as may be otherwise specified in the contract.

(9) Unless otherwise specified in the contract, the Contractor's obligation to correct or replace Government-furnished property shall be governed by the clause pertaining to Government property.

(e) Definitions.

(1) The clause at FAR 52.202-1, Definitions, is incorporated herein by reference. As used in this clause –

(i) Direct materials means those materials that enter directly into the end product, or that are used or consumed directly in connection with the furnishing of the end product or service.

(ii) Hourly rate means the rate(s) prescribed in the contract for payment for labor that meets the labor category qualifications of a labor category specified in the contract that are –

(A) Performed by the contractor;

(B) Performed by the subcontractors; or

(C) Transferred between divisions, subsidiaries, or affiliates of the contractor under a common control.

(iii) Materials means –

(A) Direct materials, including supplies transferred between divisions, subsidiaries, or affiliates of the contractor under a common control;

(B) Subcontracts for supplies and incidental services for which there is not a labor category specified in the contract;

(C) Other direct costs (e.g., incidental services for which there is not a labor category specified in the contract, travel, computer usage charges, etc.);

(D) The following subcontracts for services which are specifically excluded from the hourly rate: [Insert any subcontracts for services to be excluded from the hourly rates prescribed in the schedule.]; and

(E) Indirect costs specifically provided for in this clause.

(iv) Subcontract means any contract, as defined in FAR Subpart 2.1, entered into with a subcontractor to furnish supplies or services for performance of the prime contract or a subcontract including transfers between divisions, subsidiaries, or affiliates of a contractor or subcontractor. It includes, but is not limited to, purchase orders, and changes and modifications to purchase orders.

(i) Payments.

(1) Services accepted. Payment shall be made for services accepted by the Government that have been delivered to the delivery destination(s) set forth in this contract. The Government will pay the Contractor as follows upon the submission of commercial invoices approved by the Contracting Officer:

(i) Hourly rate.

(A) The amounts shall be computed by multiplying the appropriate hourly rates prescribed in the contract by the number of direct labor hours performed. Fractional parts of an hour shall be payable on a prorated basis.

(B) The rates shall be paid for all labor performed on the contract that meets the labor qualifications specified in the contract. Labor hours incurred to perform tasks for which labor qualifications were specified in the contract will not be paid to the extent the work is performed by individuals that do not meet the qualifications specified in the contract, unless specifically authorized by the Contracting Officer.

(C) Invoices may be submitted once each month (or at more frequent intervals, if approved by the Contracting Officer) to the Contracting Officer or the authorized representative.

(D) When requested by the Contracting Officer or the authorized representative, the Contractor shall substantiate invoices (including any subcontractor hours reimbursed at the hourly rate in the schedule) by evidence of actual payment, individual daily job timecards, records that verify the employees meet the qualifications for the labor categories specified in the contract, or other substantiation specified in the contract.

(E) Unless the Schedule prescribes otherwise, the hourly rates in the Schedule shall not be varied by virtue of the Contractor having performed work on an overtime basis.

(1) If no overtime rates are provided in the Schedule and the Contracting Officer approves overtime work in advance, overtime rates shall be negotiated.

(2) Failure to agree upon these overtime rates shall be treated as a dispute under the Disputes clause of this contract.

(3) If the Schedule provides rates for overtime, the premium portion of those rates will be reimbursable only to the extent the overtime is approved by the Contracting Officer.

(ii) Materials.

(A) If the Contractor furnishes materials that meet the definition of a commercial item at FAR 2.101, the price to be paid for such materials shall be the contractor's established catalog or market price, adjusted to reflect the –

(1) Quantities being acquired; and

(2) Any modifications necessary because of contract requirements.

(B) Except as provided for in paragraph (i)(1)(ii)(A) and (D)(2) of this clause, the Government will reimburse the Contractor the actual cost of materials (less any rebates, refunds, or discounts received by the contractor that are identifiable to the contract) provided the Contractor –

(1) Has made payments for materials in accordance with the terms and conditions of the agreement or invoice; or

(2) Makes these payments within 30 days of the submission of the Contractor's payment request to the Government and such payment is in accordance with the terms and conditions of the agreement or invoice.

(C) To the extent able, the Contractor shall –

(1) Obtain materials at the most advantageous prices available with due regard to securing prompt delivery of satisfactory materials; and

(2) Give credit to the Government for cash and trade discounts, rebates, scrap, commissions, and other amounts that are identifiable to the contract.

(D) Other Costs. Unless listed below, other direct and indirect costs will not be reimbursed.

(1) Other Direct Costs. The Government will reimburse the Contractor on the basis of actual cost for the following, provided such costs comply with the requirements in paragraph (i)(1)(ii)(B) of this clause: [Insert each element of other direct costs (e.g., travel, computer usage charges, etc. Insert "None" if no reimbursement for other direct costs will be provided. If this is an indefinite delivery contract, the Contracting Officer may insert "Each order must list separately the elements of other direct charge(s) for that order or, if no reimbursement for other direct costs will be provided, insert 'None'."]

(2) Indirect Costs (Material Handling, Subcontract Administration, etc.). The Government will reimburse the Contractor for indirect costs on a pro-rata basis over the period of contract performance at the following fixed price: [Insert a fixed amount for the indirect costs and payment schedule. Insert "$0" if no fixed price reimbursement for indirect costs will be provided. (If this is an indefinite delivery contract, the Contracting Officer may insert "Each order must list separately the fixed amount for the indirect costs and payment schedule or, if no reimbursement for indirect costs, insert 'None')."]

(2) Total cost. It is estimated that the total cost to the Government for the performance of this contract shall not exceed the ceiling price set forth in the Schedule and the Contractor agrees to use its best efforts to perform the work specified in the Schedule and all obligations under this contract within such ceiling price. If at any time the Contractor has reason to believe that the hourly rate payments and material costs that will accrue in performing this contract in the next succeeding 30 days, if added to all other payments and costs previously accrued, will exceed 85 percent of the ceiling price in the Schedule, the Contractor shall notify the Contracting Officer giving a

revised estimate of the total price to the Government for performing this contract with supporting reasons and documentation. If at any time during the performance of this contract, the Contractor has reason to believe that the total price to the Government for performing this contract will be substantially greater or less than the then stated ceiling price, the Contractor shall so notify the Contracting Officer, giving a revised estimate of the total price for performing this contract, with supporting reasons and documentation. If at any time during performance of this contract, the Government has reason to believe that the work to be required in performing this contract will be substantially greater or less than the stated ceiling price, the Contracting Officer will so advise the Contractor, giving the then revised estimate of the total amount of effort to be required under the contract.

(3) Ceiling price. The Government will not be obligated to pay the Contractor any amount in excess of the ceiling price in the Schedule, and the Contractor shall not be obligated to continue performance if to do so would exceed the ceiling price set forth in the Schedule, unless and until the Contracting Officer notifies the Contractor in writing that the ceiling price has been increased and specifies in the notice a revised ceiling that shall constitute the ceiling price for performance under this contract. When and to the extent that the ceiling price set forth in the Schedule has been increased, any hours expended and material costs incurred by the Contractor in excess of the ceiling price before the increase shall be allowable to the same extent as if the hours expended and material costs had been incurred after the increase in the ceiling price.

(4) Access to records. At any time before final payment under this contract, the Contracting Officer (or authorized representative) will have access to the following (access shall be limited to the listing below unless otherwise agreed to by the Contractor and the Contracting Officer):

(i) Records that verify that the employees whose time has been included in any invoice meet the qualifications for the labor categories specified in the contract;

(ii) For labor hours (including any subcontractor hours reimbursed at the hourly rate in the schedule), when timecards are required as substantiation for payment –

(A) The original timecards (paper-based or electronic);

(B) The Contractor's timekeeping procedures;

(C) Contractor records that show the distribution of labor between jobs or contracts; and

(D) Employees whose time has been included in any invoice for the purpose of verifying that these employees have worked the hours shown on the invoices.

(iii) For material and subcontract costs that are reimbursed on the basis of actual cost –

(A) Any invoices or subcontract agreements substantiating material costs; and

(B) Any documents supporting payment of those invoices.

(5) Overpayments/Underpayments. Each payment previously made shall be subject to reduction to the extent of amounts, on preceding invoices, that are found by the Contracting Officer not to have been properly payable and shall also be subject to reduction for overpayments or to

increase for underpayments. The Contractor shall promptly pay any such reduction within 30 days unless the parties agree otherwise. The Government within 30 days will pay any such increases, unless the parties agree otherwise. The Contractor's payment will be made by check. If the Contractor becomes aware of a duplicate invoice payment or that the Government has otherwise overpaid on an invoice payment, the Contractor shall –

(i) Remit the overpayment amount to the payment office cited in the contract along with a description of the overpayment including the –

(A) Circumstances of the overpayment (e.g., duplicate payment, erroneous payment, liquidation errors, date(s) of overpayment);

(B) Affected contract number and delivery order number, if applicable;

(C) Affected contract line item or subline item, if applicable; and

(D) Contractor point of contact.

(ii) Provide a copy of the remittance and supporting documentation to the Contracting Officer.

(6)

(i) All amounts that become payable by the Contractor to the Government under this contract shall bear simple interest from the date due until paid unless paid within 30 days of becoming due. The interest rate shall be the interest rate established by the Secretary of the Treasury, as provided in section 611 of the Contract Disputes Act of 1978 (Public Law 95-563), which is applicable to the period in which the amount becomes due, and then at the rate applicable for each six month period as established by the Secretary until the amount is paid.

(ii) The Government may issue a demand for payment to the Contractor upon finding a debt is due under the contract.

(iii) Final Decisions. The Contracting Officer will issue a final decision as required by 33.211 if –

(A) The Contracting Officer and the Contractor are unable to reach agreement on the existence or amount of a debt in a timely manner;

(B) The Contractor fails to liquidate a debt previously demanded by the Contracting Officer within the timeline specified in the demand for payment unless the amounts were not repaid because the Contractor has requested an installment payment agreement; or

(C) The Contractor requests a deferment of collection on a debt previously demanded by the Contracting Officer (see FAR 32.607-2).

(iv) If a demand for payment was previously issued for the debt, the demand for payment included in the final decision shall identify the same due date as the original demand for payment.

(v) Amounts shall be due at the earliest of the following dates:

(A) The date fixed under this contract.

(B) The date of the first written demand for payment, including any demand for payment resulting from a default termination.

(vi) The interest charge shall be computed for the actual number of calendar days involved beginning on the due date and ending on –

(A) The date on which the designated office receives payment from the Contractor;

(B) The date of issuance of a Government check to the Contractor from which an amount otherwise payable has been withheld as a credit against the contract debt; or

(C) The date on which an amount withheld and applied to the contract debt would otherwise have become payable to the Contractor.

(vii) The interest charge made under this clause may be reduced under the procedures prescribed in 32.608-2 of the Federal Acquisition Regulation in effect on the date of this contract.

(viii) Upon receipt and approval of the invoice designated by the Contractor as the "completion invoice" and supporting documentation, and upon compliance by the Contractor with all terms of this contract, any outstanding balances will be paid within 30 days unless the parties agree otherwise. The completion invoice, and supporting documentation, shall be submitted by the Contractor as promptly as practicable following completion of the work under this contract, but in no event later than 1 year (or such longer period as the Contracting Officer may approve in writing) from the date of completion.

(7) Release of claims. The Contractor, and each assignee under an assignment entered into under this contract and in effect at the time of final payment under this contract, shall execute and deliver, at the time of and as a condition precedent to final payment under this contract, a release discharging the Government, its officers, agents, and employees of and from all liabilities, obligations, and claims arising out of or under this contract, subject only to the following exceptions.

(i) Specified claims in stated amounts, or in estimated amounts if the amounts are not susceptible to exact statement by the Contractor.

(ii) Claims, together with reasonable incidental expenses, based upon the liabilities of the Contractor to third parties arising out of performing this contract, that are not known to the Contractor on the date of the execution of the release, and of which the Contractor gives notice in writing to the Contracting Officer not more than 6 years after the date of the release or the date of any notice to the Contractor that the Government is prepared to make final payment, whichever is earlier.

(iii) Claims for reimbursement of costs (other than expenses of the Contractor by reason of its indemnification of the Government against patent liability), including reasonable incidental expenses, incurred by the Contractor under the terms of this contract relating to patents.

(8) Prompt payment. The Government will make payment in accordance with the Prompt Payment Act (31 U.S.C. 3903) and prompt payment regulations at 5 CFR part 1315.

(9) Electronic Funds Transfer (EFT). If the Government makes payment by EFT, see 52.212-5(b) for the appropriate EFT clause.

(10) Discount. In connection with any discount offered for early payment, time shall be computed from the date of the invoice. For the purpose of computing the discount earned, payment shall be considered to have been made on the date that appears on the payment check or the specified payment date if an electronic funds transfer payment is made.

(l) Termination for the Government's convenience. The Government reserves the right to terminate this contract, or any part hereof, for its sole convenience. In the event of such termination, the Contractor shall immediately stop all work hereunder and shall immediately cause any and all of its suppliers and subcontractors to cease work. Subject to the terms of this contract, the Contractor shall be paid an amount for direct labor hours (as defined in the Schedule of the contract) determined by multiplying the number of direct labor hours expended before the effective date of termination by the hourly rate(s) in the contract, less any hourly rate payments already made to the Contractor plus reasonable charges the Contractor can demonstrate to the satisfaction of the Government using its standard record keeping system that have resulted from the termination. The Contractor shall not be required to comply with the cost accounting standards or contract cost principles for this purpose. This paragraph does not give the Government any right to audit the Contractor's records. The Contractor shall not be paid for any work performed or costs incurred that reasonably could have been avoided.

52.227-1 Authorization and Consent

As prescribed in 27.201-2(a)(1), insert the following clause:

AUTHORIZATION AND CONSENT (DEC 2007)

(a) The Government authorizes and consents to all use and manufacture, in performing this contract or any subcontract at any tier, of any invention described in and covered by a United States patent –

(1) Embodied in the structure or composition of any article the delivery of which is accepted by the Government under this contract; or

(2) Used in machinery, tools, or methods whose use necessarily results from compliance by the Contractor or a subcontractor with (i) specifications or written provisions forming a part of this contract or (ii) specific written instructions given by the Contracting Officer directing the manner of performance. the entire liability to the Government for infringement of a United States patent shall be determined solely by the provisions of the indemnity clause, if any, included in this contract or any subcontract hereunder (including any lower-tier subcontract), and the Government assumes liability for all other infringement to the extent of the authorization and consent hereinabove granted.

(b) The Contractor shall include the substance of this clause, including this paragraph (b), in all subcontracts that are expected to exceed the simplified acquisition threshold. However, omission of this clause from any subcontract, including those at or below the simplified acquisition threshold, does not affect this authorization and consent.

(End of clause)

Alternate I (Apr 1984). As prescribed in 27.201-2 (a)(2), substitute the following paragraph (a) for paragraph (a) of the basic clause:

(a) The Government authorizes and consents to all use and manufacture of any invention described in and covered by a United States patent in the performance of this contract or any subcontract at any tier.

Alternate II (Apr 1984). As prescribed in 27.201-2(a)(3), substitute the following paragraph (a) for paragraph (a) of the basic clause:

(a) The Government authorizes and consents to all use and manufacture in the performance of any order at any tier or subcontract at any tier placed under this contract for communication services and facilities for which rates, charges, and tariffs are not established by a government regulatory body, of any invention described in and covered by a United States patent –

(1) Embodied in the structure or composition of any article the delivery of which is accepted by the Government under this contract; or

(2) Used in machinery, tools, or methods whose use necessarily results from compliance by the Contractor or a subcontractor with specifications or written provisions forming a part of this contract or with specific written instructions given by the Contracting Officer directing the manner of performance.

52.227-2 Notice and Assistance Regarding Patent and Copyright Infringement

As prescribed in 27.201-2(b), insert the following clause:

NOTICE AND ASSISTANCE REGARDING PATENT AND COPYRIGHT INFRINGEMENT (DEC 2007)

(a) The Contractor shall report to the Contracting Officer, promptly and in reasonable written detail, each notice or claim of patent or copyright infringement based on the performance of this contract of which the Contractor has knowledge.

(b) In the event of any claim or suit against the Government on account of any alleged patent or copyright infringement arising out of the performance of this contract or out of the use of any supplies furnished or work or services performed under this contract, the Contractor shall furnish to the Government, when requested by the Contracting Officer, all evidence and information in the Contractor's possession pertaining to such claim or suit. Such evidence and information shall be furnished at the expense of the Government except where the Contractor has agreed to indemnify the Government.

(c) The Contractor shall include the substance of this clause, including this paragraph (c), in all subcontracts that are expected to exceed the simplified acquisition threshold.

(End of clause)

52.227-3 Patent Indemnity

As prescribed in 27.201-2(c)(1), insert the following clause:

PATENT INDEMNITY (APR 1984)

(a) The Contractor shall indemnify the Government and its officers, agents, and employees against liability, including costs, for infringement of any United States patent (except a patent issued upon an application that is now or may hereafter be withheld from issue pursuant to a Secrecy Order under 35 U.S.C. 181) arising out of the manufacture or delivery of supplies, the performance of services, or the construction, alteration, modification, or repair of real property (hereinafter referred to as "construction work") under this contract, or out of the use or disposal by or for the account of the Government of such supplies or construction work.

(b) This indemnity shall not apply unless the Contractor shall have been informed as soon as practicable by the Government of the suit or action alleging such infringement and shall have been given such opportunity as is afforded by applicable laws, rules, or regulations to participate in its defense. Further, this indemnity shall not apply to –

> (1) An infringement resulting from compliance with specific written instructions of the Contracting Officer directing a change in the supplies to be delivered or in the materials or equipment to be used, or directing a manner of performance of the contract not normally used by the Contractor;
>
> (2) An infringement resulting from addition to or change in supplies or components furnished or construction work performed that was made subsequent to delivery or performance; or
>
> (3) A claimed infringement that is unreasonably settled without the consent of the Contractor, unless required by final decree of a court of competent jurisdiction.

(End of clause)

Alternate I (Apr 1984). As prescribed in 27.201-2(c)(2), add the following paragraph (c) to the basic clause:

(c) This patent indemnification shall not apply to the following items:

____

[Contracting Officer list and/or identify the items to be excluded from this indemnity.]

Alternate II (Apr 1984). As prescribed in 27.201-2(c)(2), add the following paragraph (c) to the basic clause:

(c) This patent indemnification shall cover the following items:

____

[List and/or identify the items to be included under this indemnity.]

Alternate III (July 1995). As prescribed in 27.201-2(c)(3), add the following paragraph (c) to the basic clause:

(c) As to subcontracts at any tier for communication service, this clause shall apply only to individual communication service authorizations over the simplified acquisition threshold issued under this contract and covering those communications services and facilities –

(1) That are or have been sold or offered for sale by the Contractor to the public,

(2) That can be provided over commercially available equipment, or

(3) That involve relatively minor modifications.

52.227-4 Patent Indemnity – Construction Contracts

As prescribed in 27.201-2(d)(1), insert the following clause:

PATENT INDEMNITY – CONSTRUCTION CONTRACTS (DEC 2007)

Except as otherwise provided, the Contractor shall indemnify the Government and its officers, agents, and employees against liability, including costs and expenses, for infringement of any United States patent (except a patent issued upon an application that is now or may hereafter be withheld from issue pursuant to a Secrecy Order under (35 U.S.C. 181) arising out of performing this contract or out of the use or disposal by or for the account of the Government of supplies furnished or work performed under this contract.

(End of clause)

Alternate I (Dec 2007). As prescribed in 27.201-2(d)(2), designate the first paragraph of the basic clause as paragraph (a) and add the following paragraph (b) to the basic clause:

(b) This patent indemnification shall not apply to the following items:

____

[Contracting Officer list the items to be excluded.]

52.227-5 Waiver of Indemnity

As prescribed in 27.201-2(e), insert the following clause:

WAIVER OF INDEMNITY (APR 1984)

Any provision or clause of this contract to the contrary notwithstanding, the Government hereby authorizes and consents to the use and manufacture, solely in performing this contract, of any invention covered by the United States patents identified below and waives indemnification by the Contractor with respect to such patents:

____

[Contracting Officer identify the patents by number or by other means if more appropriate.]

(End of clause)

52.227-6 Royalty Information

As prescribed in 27.202-5(a)(1), insert the following provision:

ROYALTY INFORMATION (APR 1984)

(a) Cost or charges for royalties. When the response to this solicitation contains costs or charges for royalties totaling more than $250, the following information shall be included in the response relating to each separate item of royalty or license fee:

(1) Name and address of licensor.

(2) Date of license agreement.

(3) Patent numbers, patent application serial numbers, or other basis on which the royalty is payable.

(4) Brief description, including any part or model numbers of each contract item or component on which the royalty is payable.

(5) Percentage or dollar rate of royalty per unit.

(6) Unit price of contract item.

(7) Number of units.

(8) Total dollar amount of royalties.

(b) Copies of current licenses. In addition, if specifically requested by the Contracting Officer before execution of the contract, the offeror shall furnish a copy of the current license agreement and an identification of applicable claims of specific patents.

(End of provision)

Alternate I (Apr 1984). As prescribed in 27.202-5(a)(2), substitute the following for the introductory portion of paragraph (a) of the basic provision:

When the response to this solicitation covers charges for special construction or special assembly that contain costs or charges for royalties totaling more than $250, the following information shall be included in the response relating to each separate item of royalty or license fee.

52.227-7 Patents – Notice of Government Licensee.

As prescribed at 27.202-5(b), insert the following provision:

PATENTS – NOTICE OF GOVERNMENT LICENSEE (APR 1984)

The Government is obligated to pay a royalty applicable to the proposed acquisition because of a license agreement between the Government and the patent owner. The patent number is ____ [Contracting Officer fill in], and the royalty rate is ____ [Contracting Officer fill in]. If the offeror is the owner of, or a licensee under, the patent, indicate below:

- Owner o Licensee

If an offeror does not indicate that it is the owner or a licensee of the patent, its offer will be evaluated by adding thereto an amount equal to the royalty.

(End of provision)

52.227-8 [Reserved]

52.227-9 Refund of Royalties

As prescribed in 27.202-5(c), insert the following clause:

REFUND OF ROYALTIES (APR 1984)

(a) The contract price includes certain amounts for royalties payable by the Contractor or subcontractors or both, which amounts have been reported to the Contracting Officer.

(b) The term "royalties" as used in this clause refers to any costs or charges in the nature of royalties, license fees, patent or license amortization costs, or the like, for the use of or for rights in patents and patent applications in connection with performing this contract or any subcontract hereunder.

(c) The Contractor shall furnish to the Contracting Officer, before final payment under this contract, a statement of royalties paid or required to be paid in connection with performing this contract and subcontracts hereunder together with the reasons.

(d) The Contractor will be compensated for royalties reported under paragraph (c) of this clause, only to the extent that such royalties were included in the contract price and are determined by the Contracting Officer to be properly chargeable to the Government and allocable to the contract. To the extent that any royalties that are included in the contract price are not in fact paid by the Contractor or are determined by the Contracting Officer not to be properly chargeable to the Government and allocable to the contract, the contract price shall be reduced. Repayment or credit to the Government shall be made as the Contracting Officer directs.

(e) If, at any time within 3 years after final payment under this contract, the Contractor for any reason is relieved in whole or in part from the payment of the royalties included in the final contract price as adjusted pursuant to paragraph (d) of this clause, the Contractor shall promptly notify the Contracting Officer of that fact and shall reimburse the Government in a corresponding amount.

(f) The substance of this clause, including this paragraph (f), shall be included in any subcontract in which the amount of royalties reported during negotiation of the subcontract exceeds $250. (End of clause)

52.227-10 Filing of Patent Applications – Classified Subject Matter

As prescribed at 27.203-2, insert the following clause:

FILING OF PATENT APPLICATIONS – CLASSIFIED SUBJECT MATTER (DEC 2007)

(a) Before filing or causing to be filed a patent application in the United States disclosing any subject matter of this contract classified "Secret" or higher, the Contractor shall, citing the 30-day provision below, transmit the proposed application to the Contracting Officer. The Government shall determine whether, for reasons of national security, the application should be placed under an order of secrecy, sealed in accordance with the provision of 35 U.S.C. 181-188, or the issuance of a patent otherwise delayed under pertinent United States statutes or regulations. The Contractor shall observe any instructions of the Contracting Officer regarding the manner of delivery of the patent application to the United States Patent Office, but the Contractor shall not be denied the right to file the application. If the Contracting Officer shall not have given any such instructions within 30 days from the date of mailing or other transmittal of the proposed application, the Contractor may file the application.

(b) Before filing a patent application in the United States disclosing any subject matter of this contract classified "Confidential," the Contractor shall furnish to the Contracting Officer a copy of the application for Government determination whether, for reasons of national security, the application should be placed under an order of secrecy or the issuance of a patent should be otherwise delayed under pertinent United States statutes or regulations.

(c) Where the subject matter of this contract is classified for reasons of security, the Contractor shall not file, or cause to be filed, in any country other than in the United States as provided in paragraphs (a) and (b) of this clause, an application or registration for a patent containing any of the subject matter of this contract without first obtaining written approval of the Contracting Officer.

(d) When filing any patent application coming within the scope of this clause, the Contractor shall observe all applicable security regulations covering the transmission of classified subject matter and shall promptly furnish to the Contracting Officer the serial number, filing date, and name of the country of any such application. When transmitting the application to the United States Patent Office, the Contractor shall by separate letter identify by agency and number the contract or contracts that require security classification markings to be placed on the application.

(e) The Contractor shall include the substance of this clause, including this paragraph (e), in all subcontracts that cover or are likely to cover classified subject matter.

(End of clause)

52.227-11 Patent Rights – Ownership by the Contractor

As prescribed in 27.303(b)(1), insert the following clause:

PATENT RIGHTS – OWNERSHIP BY THE CONTRACTOR (DEC 2007)

(a) As used in this clause –

"Invention" means any invention or discovery that is or may be patentable or otherwise protectable under title 35 of the U.S. Code, or any variety of plant that is or may be protectable under the Plant Variety Protection Act (7 U.S.C. 2321, et seq.)

"Made" means –

> (1) When used in relation to any invention other than a plant variety, the conception or first actual reduction to practice of the invention; or
>
> (2) When used in relation to a plant variety, that the Contractor has at least tentatively determined that the variety has been reproduced with recognized characteristics.

"Nonprofit organization" means a university or other institution of higher education or an organization of the type described in section 501(c)(3) of the Internal Revenue Code of 1954 (26 U.S.C. 501(c)) and exempt from taxation under section 501(a) of the Internal Revenue Code (26 U.S.C. 501(a)), or any nonprofit scientific or educational organization qualified under a State nonprofit organization statute.

"Practical application" means to manufacture, in the case of a composition of product; to practice, in the case of a process or method; or to operate, in the case of a machine or system; and, in each case, under such conditions as to establish that the invention is being utilized and that its benefits are, to the extent permitted by law or Government regulations, available to the public on reasonable terms.

"Subject invention" means any invention of the Contractor made in the performance of work under this contract.

(b) Contractor's rights.

(1) Ownership. The Contractor may retain ownership of each subject invention throughout the world in accordance with the provisions of this clause.

(2) License.

(i) The Contractor shall retain a nonexclusive royalty-free license throughout the world in each subject invention to which the Government obtains title, unless the Contractor fails to disclose the invention within the times specified in paragraph (c) of this clause. The Contractor's license extends to any domestic subsidiaries and affiliates within the corporate structure of which the Contractor is a part, and includes the right to grant sublicenses to the extent the Contractor was legally obligated to do so at contract award. The license is transferable only with the written approval of the agency, except when transferred to the successor of that part of the Contractor's business to which the invention pertains.

(ii) The Contractor's license may be revoked or modified by the agency to the extent necessary to achieve expeditious practical application of the subject invention in a particular country in accordance with the procedures in FAR 27.302(i)(2) and 27.304-1(f).

(c) Contractor's obligations.

(1) The Contractor shall disclose in writing each subject invention to the Contracting Officer within 2 months after the inventor discloses it in writing to Contractor personnel responsible for patent matters. The disclosure shall identify the inventor(s) and this contract under which the subject invention was made. It shall be sufficiently complete in technical detail to convey a clear understanding of the subject invention. The disclosure shall also identify any publication, on sale (i.e., sale or offer for sale), or public use of the subject invention, or whether a manuscript

describing the subject invention has been submitted for publication and, if so, whether it has been accepted for publication. In addition, after disclosure to the agency, the Contractor shall promptly notify the Contracting Officer of the acceptance of any manuscript describing the subject invention for publication and any on sale or public use.

(2) The Contractor shall elect in writing whether or not to retain ownership of any subject invention by notifying the Contracting Officer within 2 years of disclosure to the agency. However, in any case where publication, on sale, or public use has initiated the 1-year statutory period during which valid patent protection can be obtained in the United States, the period for election of title may be shortened by the agency to a date that is no more than 60 days prior to the end of the statutory period.

(3) The Contractor shall file either a provisional or a nonprovisional patent application or a Plant Variety Protection Application on an elected subject invention within 1 year after election. However, in any case where a publication, on sale, or public use has initiated the 1-year statutory period during which valid patent protection can be obtained in the United States, the Contractor shall file the application prior to the end of that statutory period. If the Contractor files a provisional application, it shall file a nonprovisional application within 10 months of the filing of the provisional application. The Contractor shall file patent applications in additional countries or international patent offices within either 10 months of the first filed patent application (whether provisional or nonprovisional) or 6 months from the date permission is granted by the Commissioner of Patents to file foreign patent applications where such filing has been prohibited by a Secrecy Order.

(4) The Contractor may request extensions of time for disclosure, election, or filing under paragraphs (c)(1), (c)(2), and (c)(3) of this clause.

(d) Government's rights –

(1) Ownership. The Contractor shall assign to the agency, on written request, title to any subject invention –

(i) If the Contractor fails to disclose or elect ownership to the subject invention within the times specified in paragraph (c) of this clause, or elects not to retain ownership; provided, that the agency may request title only within 60 days after learning of the Contractor's failure to disclose or elect within the specified times.

(ii) In those countries in which the Contractor fails to file patent applications within the times specified in paragraph (c) of this clause; provided, however, that if the Contractor has filed a patent application in a country after the times specified in paragraph (c) of this clause, but prior to its receipt of the written request of the agency, the Contractor shall continue to retain ownership in that country.

(iii) In any country in which the Contractor decides not to continue the prosecution of any application for, to pay the maintenance fees on, or defend in reexamination or opposition proceeding on, a patent on a subject invention.

(2) License. If the Contractor retains ownership of any subject invention, the Government shall have a nonexclusive, nontransferable, irrevocable, paid-up license to practice, or have practiced for or on its behalf, the subject invention throughout the world.

(e) Contractor action to protect the Government's interest.

(1) The Contractor shall execute or have executed and promptly deliver to the agency all instruments necessary to –

(i) Establish or confirm the rights the Government has throughout the world in those subject inventions in which the Contractor elects to retain ownership; and

(ii) Assign title to the agency when requested under paragraph (d) of this clause and to enable the Government to obtain patent protection and plant variety protection for that subject invention in any country.

(2) The Contractor shall require, by written agreement, its employees, other than clerical and nontechnical employees, to disclose promptly in writing to personnel identified as responsible for the administration of patent matters and in the Contractor's format, each subject invention in order that the Contractor can comply with the disclosure provisions of paragraph (c) of this clause, and to execute all papers necessary to file patent applications on subject inventions and to establish the Government's rights in the subject inventions. The disclosure format should require, as a minimum, the information required by paragraph (c)(1) of this clause. The Contractor shall instruct such employees, through employee agreements or other suitable educational programs, as to the importance of reporting inventions in sufficient time to permit the filing of patent applications prior to U.S. or foreign statutory bars.

(3) The Contractor shall notify the Contracting Officer of any decisions not to file a nonprovisional patent application, continue the prosecution of a patent application, pay maintenance fees, or defend in a reexamination or opposition proceeding on a patent, in any country, not less than 30 days before the expiration of the response or filing period required by the relevant patent office.

(4) The Contractor shall include, within the specification of any United States nonprovisional patent or plant variety protection application and any patent or plant variety protection certificate issuing thereon covering a subject invention, the following statement, "This invention was made with Government support under (identify the contract) awarded by (identify the agency). The Government has certain rights in the invention."

(f) Reporting on utilization of subject inventions. The Contractor shall submit, on request, periodic reports no more frequently than annually on the utilization of a subject invention or on efforts at obtaining utilization of the subject invention that are being made by the Contractor or its licensees or assignees. The reports shall include information regarding the status of development, date of first commercial sale or use, gross royalties received by the Contractor, and other data and information as the agency may reasonably specify. The Contractor also shall provide additional reports as may be requested by the agency in connection with any march-in proceeding undertaken by the agency in accordance with paragraph (h) of this clause. The Contractor also shall mark any utilization report as confidential/proprietary to help prevent inadvertent release outside the Government. As required by 35 U.S.C. 202(c)(5), the agency will not disclose that information to persons outside the Government without the Contractor's permission.

(g) Preference for United States industry. Notwithstanding any other provision of this clause, neither the Contractor nor any assignee shall grant to any person the exclusive right to use or sell any subject invention in the United States unless the person agrees that any products embodying the subject invention or produced through the use of the subject invention will be manufactured substantially in the United States. However, in individual cases, the requirement for an agreement may be waived by the agency upon a showing by the Contractor or its assignee that reasonable but unsuccessful efforts have been made to grant licenses on similar terms to potential licensees that would be likely to manufacture substantially in the United States, or that under the circumstances domestic manufacture is not commercially feasible.

(h) March-in rights. The Contractor acknowledges that, with respect to any subject invention in which it has retained ownership, the agency has the right to require licensing pursuant to 35 U.S.C. 203 and 210(c), and in accordance with the procedures in 37 CFR 401.6 and any supplemental regulations of the agency in effect on the date of contract award.

(i) Special provisions for contracts with nonprofit organizations. If the Contractor is a nonprofit organization, it shall –

> (1) Not assign rights to a subject invention in the United States without the written approval of the agency, except where an assignment is made to an organization that has as one of its primary functions the management of inventions, provided, that

the assignee shall be subject to the same provisions as the Contractor;

(2) Share royalties collected on a subject invention with the inventor, including Federal employee co-inventors (but through their agency if the agency deems it appropriate) when the subject invention is assigned in accordance with 35 U.S.C. 202(e) and 37 CFR 401.10;

(3) Use the balance of any royalties or income earned by the Contractor with respect to subject inventions, after payment of expenses (including payments to inventors) incidental to the administration of subject inventions for the support of scientific research or education; and

(4) Make efforts that are reasonable under the circumstances to attract licensees of subject inventions that are small business concerns, and give a preference to a small business concern when licensing a subject invention if the Contractor determines that the small business concern has a plan or proposal for marketing the invention which, if executed, is equally as likely to bring the invention to practical application as any plans or proposals from applicants that are not small business concerns; provided, that the Contractor is also satisfied that the small business concern has the capability and resources to carry out its plan or proposal. The decision whether to give a preference in any specific case will be at the discretion of the Contractor.

(5) Allow the Secretary of Commerce to review the Contractor's licensing program and decisions regarding small business applicants, and negotiate changes to its licensing policies, procedures, or practices with the Secretary of Commerce when the Secretary's review discloses that the Contractor could take reasonable steps to more effectively implement the requirements of paragraph (i)(4) of this clause.

(j) Communications. [Complete according to agency instructions.]

(k) Subcontracts.

(1) The Contractor shall include the substance of this clause, including this paragraph (k), in all subcontracts for experimental, developmental, or research work to be performed by a small business concern or nonprofit organization.

(2) The Contractor shall include in all other subcontracts for experimental, developmental, or research work the substance of the patent rights clause required by FAR Subpart 27.3.

(3) At all tiers, the patent rights clause must be modified to identify the parties as follows: references to the Government are not changed, and the subcontractor has all rights and obligations of the Contractor in the clause. The Contractor shall not, as part of the consideration for awarding the subcontract, obtain rights in the subcontractor's subject inventions.

(4) In subcontracts, at any tier, the agency, the subcontractor, and the Contractor agree that the mutual obligations of the parties created by this clause constitute a contract between the subcontractor and the agency with respect to the matters covered by the clause; provided, however, that nothing in this paragraph is intended to confer any jurisdiction under the Contract Disputes Act in connection with proceedings under paragraph (h) of this clause.

(End of clause)

Alternate I (Jun 1989). As prescribed in 27.303(b)(3), add the following sentence at the end of paragraph (d)(2) of the basic clause:

The license shall include the right of the Government to sublicense foreign governments, their nationals and international organizations pursuant to the following treaties or international agreements: ______________________* [*Contracting Officer complete with the names of applicable existing treaties or international agreements. The above language is not intended to apply to treaties or agreements that are in effect on the date of the award but are not listed.]

Alternate II (Dec 2007). As prescribed in 27.303(b)(4), add the following sentence at the end of paragraph (d)(2) of the basic clause:

The agency reserves the right to unilaterally amend this contract to identify specific treaties or international agreements entered into by the Government before or after the effective date of the contract and effectuate those license or other rights that are necessary for the Government to meet its obligations to foreign governments, their nationals, and international organizations under the treaties or international agreements with respect to subject inventions made after the date of the amendment.

Alternate III (Jun 1989). As prescribed in 27.303(b)(5), substitute the following paragraph (i)(3) in place of paragraph (i)(3) of the basic clause:

> (3) After payment of patenting costs, licensing costs, payments to inventors, and other expenses incidental to the administration of subject inventions, the balance of any royalties or income earned and retained by the Contractor during any fiscal year on subject inventions under this or any successor contract containing the same requirement, up to any amount equal to 5 percent of the budget of the facility for that fiscal year, shall be used by the Contractor for the scientific research, development, and education consistent with the research and development mission and objectives of the facility, including activities that increase the licensing potential of other inventions of the facility. If the balance exceeds 5 percent, 75 percent of the excess above 5 percent shall be paid by the Contractor to the Treasury of the United States and the remaining 25 percent shall be used by the Contractor only for the same purposes as described above. To the extent it provides the most effective technology transfer, the licensing of subject inventions shall be administered by Contractor employees on location at the facility.

Alternate IV (Jun 1989). As prescribed in 27.303(b)(6), include the following paragraph (e)(5) in paragraph (e) of the basic clause:

> (5) The Contractor shall establish and maintain active and effective procedures to ensure that subject inventions are promptly identified and timely disclosed, and shall submit a description of

the procedures to the Contracting Officer so that the Contracting Officer may evaluate and determine their effectiveness.

Alternate V (Dec 2007). As prescribed in 27.303(b)(7), include the following paragraph (d)(3) in paragraph (d) of the basic clause:

(d)

(3) CRADA licensing. If the Contractor performs services at a Government owned and operated laboratory or at a Government owned and Contractor operated laboratory directed by the Government to fulfill the Government's obligations under a Cooperative Research and Development Agreement (CRADA) authorized by 15 U.S.C. 3710a, the Government may require the Contractor to negotiate an agreement with the CRADA collaborating party or parties regarding the allocation of rights to any subject invention the Contractor makes, solely or jointly, under the CRADA. The agreement shall be negotiated prior to the Contractor undertaking the CRADA work or, with the permission of the Government, upon the identification of a subject invention. In the absence of such an agreement, the Contractor agrees to grant the collaborating party or parties an option for a license in its inventions of the same scope and terms set forth in the CRADA for inventions made by the Government.

52.227-12 [Reserved]

52.227-13 Patent Rights – Ownership by the Government

As prescribed at 27.303(e), insert the following clause:

PATENT RIGHTS – OWNERSHIP BY THE GOVERNMENT (DEC 2007)

(a) Definitions. As used in this clause –

"Invention" means any invention or discovery that is or may be patentable or otherwise protectable under title 35 of the U.S. Code or any variety of plant that is or may be protectable under the Plant Variety Protection Act (7 U.S.C. 2321, et seq.)

"Made" means –

(1) When used in relation to any invention other than a plant variety, means the conception or first actual reduction to practice of the invention; or

(2) When used in relation to a plant variety, means that the Contractor has at least tentatively determined that the variety has been reproduced with recognized characteristics.

"Practical application" means to manufacture, in the case of a composition or product; to practice, in the case of a process or method; or to operate, in the case of a machine or system; and, in each case, under such conditions as to establish that the invention is being utilized and that its benefits are, to the extent permitted by law or Government regulations, available to the public on reasonable terms.

"Subject invention" means any invention of the Contractor made in the performance of work under this contract.

(b) Ownership.

(1) Assignment to the Government. The Contractor shall assign to the Government title throughout the world to each subject invention, except to the extent that rights are retained under paragraphs (b)(2) and (d) of this clause.

(2) Greater rights determinations.

(i) The Contractor, or an employee-inventor after consultation with the Contractor, may request greater rights than the nonexclusive license provided in paragraph (d) of this clause. The request for a greater rights must be submitted to the Contracting Officer at the time of the first disclosure of the subject invention pursuant to paragraph (e)(2) of this clause, or not later than 8 months thereafter, unless a longer period is authorized in writing by the Contracting Officer for good cause shown in writing by the Contractor. Each determination of greater rights under this contract normally shall be subject to paragraph (c) of this clause, and to the reservations and conditions deemed to be appropriate by the agency.

(ii) Upon request, the Contractor shall provide the filing date, serial number and title, a copy of the patent application (including an English-language version if filed in a language other than English), and patent number and issue date for any subject invention in any country for which the Contractor has retained title.

(iii) Upon request, the Contractor shall furnish the agency an irrevocable power to inspect and make copies of the patent application file.

(c) Minimum rights acquired by the Government.

(1) Regarding each subject invention to which the Contractor retains ownership, the Contractor agrees as follows:

(i) The Government will have a nonexclusive, nontransferable, irrevocable, paid-up license to practice, or have practiced for or on its behalf, the subject invention throughout the world.

(ii) The agency has the right to require licensing pursuant to 35 U.S.C. 203 and 210(c) and in accordance with the procedures set forth in 37 CFR 401.6 and any supplemental regulations of the agency in effect on the date of the contract award.

(iii) Upon request, the Contractor shall submit periodic reports no more frequently than annually on the utilization, or efforts to obtain utilization, of a subject invention by the Contractor or its licensees or assignees. The reports shall include information regarding the status of development, date of first commercial sale or use, gross royalties received by the Contractor, and any other data and information as the agency may reasonably specify. The Contractor also shall provide additional reports as may be requested by the agency in connection with any march-in proceedings undertaken by the agency in accordance with paragraph (c)(1)(ii) of this clause. To the extent data or information supplied under this section is considered by the Contractor, or its licensees, or assignees to be privileged and confidential and is so marked, the agency, to the extent permitted by law, will not disclose such information to persons outside the Government.

(iv) When licensing a subject invention, the Contractor shall –

(A) Ensure that no royalties are charged on acquisitions involving Government funds, including funds derived through a Military Assistance Program of the Government or otherwise derived through the Government;

(B) Refund any amounts received as royalty charges on a subject invention in acquisitions for, or on behalf of, the Government;

(C) Provide for this refund in any instrument transferring rights in the subject invention to any party.

(v) When transferring rights in a subject invention, the Contractor shall provide for the Government's rights set forth in paragraphs (c)(1)(i) through (c)(1)(iv) of this clause.

(2) Nothing contained in paragraph (c) of this clause shall be deemed to grant to the Government rights in any invention other than a subject invention.

(d) Minimum rights to the Contractor.

(1) The Contractor is hereby granted a revocable, nonexclusive, paid-up license in each patent application filed in any country on a subject invention and any resulting patent in which the

Government obtains title, unless the Contractor fails to disclose the subject invention within the times specified in paragraph (e)(2) of this clause. The Contractor's license extends to any of its domestic subsidiaries and affiliates within the corporate structure of which the Contractor is a part, and includes the right to grant sublicenses to the extent the Contractor was legally obligated to do so at contract award. The license is transferable only with the written approval of the agency except when transferred to the successor of that part of the Contractor's business to which the subject invention pertains.

(2) The Contractor's license may be revoked or modified by the agency to the extent necessary to achieve expeditious practical application of the subject invention in a particular country in accordance with the procedures in FAR 27.302(i)(2) and 27.304-1(f).

(3) When the Government elects not to apply for a patent in any foreign country, the Contractor retains rights in that foreign country to apply for a patent, subject to the Government's rights in paragraph (c)(1) of this clause.

(e) Invention identification, disclosures, and reports.

(1) The Contractor shall establish and maintain active and effective procedures to educate its employees in order to assure that subject inventions are promptly identified and disclosed to Contractor personnel responsible for patent matters. The procedures shall include the maintenance of laboratory notebooks or equivalent records and other records as are reasonably necessary to document the conception and/or the first actual reduction to practice of subject inventions, and records that show the procedures for identifying and disclosing subject inventions are followed. Upon request, the Contractor shall furnish the Contracting Officer a description of these procedures for evaluation and for a determination as to their effectiveness.

(2) The Contractor shall disclose in writing each subject invention to the Contracting Officer within 2 months after the inventor

discloses it in writing to Contractor personnel responsible for patent matters or, if earlier, within 6 months after the Contractor becomes aware that a subject invention has been made, but in any event before any on sale (i.e., sale or offer for sale), public use, or publication of the subject invention known to the Contractor. The disclosure shall identify the contract under which the subject invention was made and the inventor(s). It shall be sufficiently complete in technical detail to convey a clear understanding of the subject invention. The disclosure shall also identify any publication, on sale, or public use of the subject invention and whether a manuscript describing the subject invention has been submitted for publication and, if so, whether it has been accepted for publication. In addition, after disclosure to the agency, the Contractor shall promptly notify the Contracting Officer of the acceptance of any manuscript describing the subject invention for publication and any on sale or public use.

(3) The Contractor shall furnish the Contracting Officer the following:

> (i) Interim reports every 12 months (or a longer period as may be specified by the Contracting Officer) from the date of the contract, listing subject inventions during that period, and stating that all subject inventions have been disclosed (or that there are none) and that the procedures required by paragraph (e)(1) of this clause have been followed.
>
> (ii) A final report, within 3 months after completion of the contracted work, listing all subject inventions or stating that there were none, and listing all subcontracts at any tier containing a patent rights clause or stating that there were none.

(4) The Contractor shall require, by written agreement, its employees, other than clerical and nontechnical employees, to disclose promptly in writing to personnel identified as responsible for the administration of patent matters and in the Contractor's format each subject invention in order that the Contractor can

comply with the disclosure provisions of paragraph (c) of this clause, and to execute all papers necessary to file patent applications on subject inventions and to establish the Government's rights in the subject inventions. This disclosure format should require, as a minimum, the information required by paragraph (e)(2) of this clause. The Contractor shall instruct such employees, through employee agreements or other suitable educational programs, as to the importance of reporting inventions in sufficient time to permit the filing of patent applications prior to U.S. or foreign statutory bars.

(5) Subject to FAR 27.302(i), the Contractor agrees that the Government may duplicate and disclose subject invention disclosures and all other reports and papers furnished or required to be furnished pursuant to this clause.

(f) Examination of records relating to inventions.

(1) The Contracting Officer or any authorized representative shall, until 3 years after final payment under this contract, have the right to examine any books (including laboratory notebooks), records, and documents of the Contractor relating to the conception or first actual reduction to practice of inventions in the same field of technology as the work under this contract to determine whether –

(i) Any inventions are subject inventions;

(ii) The Contractor has established and maintains the procedures required by paragraphs (e)(1) and (e)(4) of this clause; and

(iii) The Contractor and its inventors have complied with the procedures.

(2) The Contractor shall disclose to the Contracting Officer, for the determination of ownership rights, any unreported invention that the Contracting Officer believes may be a subject invention.

(3) Any examination of records under paragraph (f) of this clause will be subject to appropriate conditions to protect the confidentiality of the information involved.

(g) Withholding of payment. (This paragraph does not apply to subcontracts.)

(1) Any time before final payment under this contract, the Contracting Officer may, in the Government's interest, withhold payment until a reserve not exceeding $50,000 or 5 percent of the amount of this contract, whichever is less, shall have been set aside if, in the Contracting Office's opinion, the Contractor fails to –

(i) Establish, maintain, and follow effective procedures for identifying and disclosing subject inventions pursuant to paragraph (e)(1) of this clause;

(ii) Disclose any subject invention pursuant to paragraph (e)(2) of this clause;

(iii) Deliver acceptable interim reports pursuant to paragraph (e)(3)(i) of this clause; or

(iv) Provide the information regarding subcontracts pursuant to paragraph (i)(4) of this clause.

(2) The Contracting Officer will withhold the reserve or balance until the Contracting Officer has determined that the Contractor has rectified whatever deficiencies exist and has delivered all reports, disclosures, and other information required by this clause.

(3) The Contracting Officer will not make final payment under this contract before the Contractor delivers to the Contracting Officer, as required by this clause, all disclosures of subject inventions, an acceptable final report, and all due confirmatory instruments.

(4) The Contracting Officer may decrease or increase the sums withheld up to the maximum authorized. The Contracting Officer will not withhold any amount under this paragraph while the amount specified by this paragraph is being withheld under other

provisions of the contract. The withholding of any amount or the subsequent payment shall not be construed as a waiver of any Government rights.

(h) Preference for United States industry. Unless provided otherwise, neither the Contractor nor any assignee shall grant to any person the exclusive right to use or sell any subject invention in the United States unless the person agrees that any products embodying the subject invention or produced through the use of the subject invention will be manufactured substantially in the United States. However, in individual cases, the requirement may be waived by the agency upon a showing by the Contractor or assignee that reasonable but unsuccessful efforts have been made to grant licenses on similar terms to potential licensees that would be likely to manufacture substantially in the United States or that, under the circumstances, domestic manufacture is not commercially feasible.

(i) Subcontracts.

(1) The Contractor shall include the substance of the patent rights clause required by FAR Subpart 27.3 in all subcontracts for experimental, developmental, or research work. The prescribed patent rights clause must be modified to identify the parties as follows: references to the Government are not changed, and the subcontractor has all rights and obligations of the Contractor in the clause. The Contractor shall not, as part of the consideration for awarding the subcontract, obtain rights in the subcontractor's subject inventions.

(2) In the event of a refusal by a prospective subcontractor to accept the clause, the Contractor –

(i) Shall promptly submit a written notice to the Contracting Officer setting forth the subcontractor's reasons for such refusal and other pertinent information that may expedite disposition of the matter; and

(ii) Shall not proceed with such subcontract without the written authorization of the Contracting Officer.

(3) In subcontracts at any tier, the agency, the subcontractor, and the Contractor agree that the mutual obligations of the parties created by the patent rights clause constitute a contract between the subcontractor and the agency with respect to those matters covered by this clause.

(4) The Contractor shall promptly notify the Contracting Officer in writing upon the award of any subcontract at any tier containing a patent rights clause by identifying the subcontractor, the applicable patent rights clause, the work to be performed under the subcontract, and the dates of award and estimated completion. Upon request of the Contracting Officer, the Contractor shall furnish a copy of such subcontract, and, no more frequently than annually, a listing of the subcontracts that have been awarded.

(End of clause)

Alternate I (Jun 1989). As prescribed in 27.303(e) (4), add the following sentence at the end of paragraph (c)(1)(i) of the basic clause:

The license will include the right of the Government to sublicense foreign governments, their nationals, and international organizations pursuant to the following treaties or international agreements: ____________________* [*Contracting Officer complete with the names of applicable existing treaties or international agreements. The above language is not intended to apply to treaties or agreements that are in effect on the date of the award but are not listed.]

Alternate II (Dec 2007). As prescribed in 27.303(e)(5), add the following sentence at the end of paragraph (c)(1)(i) of the basic clause:

The agency reserves the right to unilaterally amend this contract to identify specific treaties or international agreements entered into by the Government before or after the effective date of this contract, and effectuate those license or other rights that are necessary for the Government to meet its obligations to foreign governments, their nationals, and international organizations under treaties or international agreements with respect to subject inventions made after the date of the amendment.

52.227-14 Rights in Data – General

As prescribed in 27.409(b)(1), insert the following clause with any appropriate alternates:

RIGHTS IN DATA – GENERAL (DEC 2007)

(a) Definitions. As used in this clause –

"Computer database" or "database means" a collection of recorded information in a form capable of, and for the purpose of, being stored in, processed, and operated on by a computer. The term does not include computer software.

"Computer software" –

(1) Means

(i) Computer programs that comprise a series of instructions, rules, routines, or statements, regardless of the media in which recorded, that allow or cause a computer to perform a specific operation or series of operations; and

(ii) Recorded information comprising source code listings, design details, algorithms, processes, flow charts, formulas, and related material that would enable the computer program to be produced, created, or compiled.

(2) Does not include computer databases or computer software documentation.

"Computer software documentation" means owner's manuals, user's manuals, installation instructions, operating instructions, and other similar items, regardless of storage medium, that explain the capabilities of the computer software or provide instructions for using the software.

"Data" means recorded information, regardless of form or the media on which it may be recorded. The term includes technical data and computer software. The term does not include information incidental to contract administration, such as financial, administrative, cost or pricing, or management information.

"Form, fit, and function data" means data relating to items, components, or processes that are sufficient to enable physical and functional interchangeability, and data identifying source, size, configuration, mating and attachment characteristics, functional characteristics, and performance requirements. For computer software it means data identifying source, functional characteristics, and performance requirements but specifically excludes the source code, algorithms, processes, formulas, and flow charts of the software.

"Limited rights" means the rights of the Government in limited rights data as set forth in the Limited Rights Notice of paragraph (g)(3) if included in this clause.

"Limited rights data" means data, other than computer software, that embody trade secrets or are commercial or financial and confidential or privileged, to the extent that such data pertain to items, components, or processes developed at private expense, including minor modifications.

"Restricted computer software" means computer software developed at private expense and that is a trade secret, is commercial or financial and confidential or privileged, or is copyrighted computer software, including minor modifications of the computer software.

"Restricted rights," as used in this clause, means the rights of the Government in restricted computer software, as set forth in a Restricted Rights Notice of paragraph (g) if included in this clause, or as otherwise may be provided in a collateral agreement incorporated in and made part of this contract, including minor modifications of such computer software.

"Technical data" means recorded information (regardless of the form or method of the recording) of a scientific or technical nature (including computer databases and computer software documentation). This term does not include computer software or financial, administrative, cost or pricing, or management data or other information incidental to contract administration. The term includes recorded information of a scientific or technical nature that is included in computer databases (See 41 U.S.C. 403(8)).

"Unlimited rights" means the rights of the Government to use, disclose, reproduce, prepare derivative works, distribute copies to the public, and perform publicly and display publicly, in any manner and for any purpose, and to have or permit others to do so.

(b) Allocation of rights.

(1) Except as provided in paragraph (c) of this clause, the Government shall have unlimited rights in –

(i) Data first produced in the performance of this contract;

(ii) Form, fit, and function data delivered under this contract;

(iii) Data delivered under this contract (except for restricted computer software) that constitute manuals or instructional and training material for installation, operation, or routine maintenance and repair of items, components, or processes delivered or furnished for use under this contract; and

(iv) All other data delivered under this contract unless provided otherwise for limited rights data or restricted computer software in accordance with paragraph (g) of this clause.

(2) The Contractor shall have the right to –

(i) Assert copyright in data first produced in the performance of this contract to the extent provided in paragraph (c)(1) of this clause;

(ii) Use, release to others, reproduce, distribute, or publish any data first produced or specifically used by the Contractor in the performance of this contract, unless provided otherwise in paragraph (d) of this clause;

(iii) Substantiate the use of, add, or correct limited rights, restricted rights, or copyright notices and to take other appropriate action, in accordance with paragraphs (e) and (f) of this clause; and

(iv) Protect from unauthorized disclosure and use those data that are limited rights data or restricted computer software to the extent provided in paragraph (g) of this clause.

(c) Copyright –

(1) Data first produced in the performance of this contract.

(i) Unless provided otherwise in paragraph (d) of this clause, the Contractor may, without prior approval of the Contracting Officer, assert copyright in scientific and technical articles based on or containing data first produced in the performance of this contract and published in academic, technical or professional journals, symposia proceedings, or similar works. The prior, express written permission of the Contracting Officer is required to assert copyright in all other data first produced in the performance of this contract.

(ii) When authorized to assert copyright to the data, the Contractor shall affix the applicable copyright notices of 17 U.S.C. 401 or 402, and an acknowledgment of Government sponsorship (including contract number).

(iii) For data other than computer software, the Contractor grants to the Government, and others acting on its behalf, a paid-up, nonexclusive, irrevocable, worldwide license in such copyrighted data to reproduce, prepare derivative works, distribute copies to the public, and perform publicly and display publicly by or on behalf of the Government. For computer software, the Contractor grants to the Government, and others acting on its behalf, a paid-up, nonexclusive, irrevocable, worldwide license in such copyrighted computer software to reproduce, prepare derivative works, and perform publicly and display publicly (but not to distribute copies to the public) by or on behalf of the Government.

(2) Data not first produced in the performance of this contract. The Contractor shall not, without the prior written permission of the Contracting Officer, incorporate in data delivered under this contract any data not first produced in the performance of this contract unless the Contractor –

(i) Identifies the data; and

(ii) Grants to the Government, or acquires on its behalf, a license of the same scope as set forth in paragraph (c)(1) of this clause or, if such data are restricted computer software, the Government shall acquire a copyright license as set forth in paragraph (g)(4) of this clause (if included in this contract) or as otherwise provided in a collateral agreement incorporated in or made part of this contract.

(3) Removal of copyright notices. The Government will not remove any authorized copyright notices placed on data pursuant to this paragraph (c), and will include such notices on all reproductions of the data.

(d) Release, publication, and use of data. The Contractor shall have the right to use, release to others, reproduce, distribute, or publish any data first produced or specifically used by the Contractor in the performance of this contract, except –

(1) As prohibited by Federal law or regulation (e.g., export control or national security laws or regulations);

(2) As expressly set forth in this contract; or

(3) If the Contractor receives or is given access to data necessary for the performance of this contract that contain restrictive markings, the Contractor shall treat the data in accordance with

such markings unless specifically authorized otherwise in writing by the Contracting Officer.

(e) Unauthorized marking of data.

(1) Notwithstanding any other provisions of this contract concerning inspection or acceptance, if any data delivered under this contract are marked with the notices specified in paragraph (g)(3) or (g) (4) if included in this clause, and use of the notices is not authorized by this clause, or if the data bears any other restrictive or limiting markings not authorized by this contract, the Contracting Officer may at any time either return the data to the Contractor, or cancel or ignore the markings. However, pursuant to 41 U.S.C. 253d, the following procedures shall apply prior to canceling or ignoring the markings.

(i) The Contracting Officer will make written inquiry to the Contractor affording the Contractor 60 days from receipt of the inquiry to provide written justification to substantiate the propriety of the markings;

(ii) If the Contractor fails to respond or fails to provide written justification to substantiate the propriety of the markings within the 60-day period (or a longer time approved in writing by the Contracting Officer for good cause shown), the Government shall have the right to cancel or ignore the markings at any time after said period and the data will no longer be made subject to any disclosure prohibitions.

(iii) If the Contractor provides written justification to substantiate the propriety of the markings within the period set in paragraph (e)(1)(i) of this clause, the Contracting Officer will consider such written justification and determine whether or not the markings are to be cancelled or ignored. If the Contracting Officer determines that the markings are authorized, the Contractor will be so notified in writing. If the Contracting Officer determines, with concurrence of the head of the contracting activity, that the markings are not authorized, the Contracting Officer will furnish the Contractor a written determination, which determination will become the final agency decision regarding the appropriateness of the markings unless the Contractor files suit in a court of competent jurisdiction within 90 days of receipt of the Contracting Officer's decision. The Government will continue to abide by the markings under this paragraph (e)(1)(iii) until final resolution of the matter either by the Contracting Officer's determination becoming final (in which instance the Government will thereafter have the right to cancel or ignore the markings at any time and the data will no longer be made subject to any disclosure prohibitions), or by final disposition of the matter by court decision if suit is filed.

(2) The time limits in the procedures set forth in paragraph (e)(1) of this clause may be modified in accordance with agency regulations implementing the Freedom of Information Act (5 U.S.C. 552) if necessary to respond to a request thereunder.

(3) Except to the extent the Government's action occurs as the result of final disposition of the matter by a court of competent jurisdiction, the Contractor is not precluded by paragraph (e) of the clause from bringing a claim, in accordance with the Disputes clause of this contract, that may arise as the result of the Government removing or ignoring authorized markings on data delivered under this contract.

(f) Omitted or incorrect markings.

(1) Data delivered to the Government without any restrictive markings shall be deemed to have been furnished with unlimited rights. The Government is not liable for the disclosure, use, or reproduction of such data.

(2) If the unmarked data has not been disclosed without restriction outside the Government, the Contractor may request, within 6 months (or a longer time approved by the Contracting Officer in

writing for good cause shown) after delivery of the data, permission to have authorized notices placed on the data at the Contractor's expense. The Contracting Officer may agree to do so if the Contractor –

(i) Identifies the data to which the omitted notice is to be applied;

(ii) Demonstrates that the omission of the notice was inadvertent;

(iii) Establishes that the proposed notice is authorized; and

(iv) Acknowledges that the Government has no liability for the disclosure, use, or reproduction of any data made prior to the addition of the notice or resulting from the omission of the notice.

(3) If data has been marked with an incorrect notice, the Contracting Officer may –

(i) Permit correction of the notice at the Contractor's expense if the Contractor identifies the data and demonstrates that the correct notice is authorized; or

(ii) Correct any incorrect notices.

(g) Protection of limited rights data and restricted computer software.

(1) The Contractor may withhold from delivery qualifying limited rights data or restricted computer software that are not data identified in paragraphs (b)(1)(i), (ii), and (iii) of this clause. As a condition to this withholding, the Contractor shall –

(i) Identify the data being withheld; and

(ii) Furnish form, fit, and function data instead.

(2) Limited rights data that are formatted as a computer database for delivery to the Government shall be treated as limited rights data and not restricted computer software.

(3) [Reserved]

(h) Subcontracting. The Contractor shall obtain from its subcontractors all data and rights therein necessary to fulfill the Contractor's obligations to the Government under this contract. If a subcontractor refuses to accept terms affording the Government those rights, the Contractor shall promptly notify the Contracting Officer of the refusal and shall not proceed with the subcontract award without authorization in writing from the Contracting Officer.

(i) Relationship to patents or other rights. Nothing contained in this clause shall imply a license to the Government under any patent or be construed as affecting the scope of any license or other right otherwise granted to the Government.

(End of clause)

Alternate I (Dec 2007). As prescribed in 27.409(b)(2), substitute the following definition for "limited rights data" in paragraph (a) of the basic clause:

"Limited rights data" means data, other than computer software, developed at private expense that embody trade secrets or are commercial or financial and confidential or privileged.

Alternate II (Dec 2007). As prescribed in 27.409(b)(3), insert the following paragraph (g)(3) in the basic clause:

(g)(3) Notwithstanding paragraph (g)(1) of this clause, the contract may identify and specify the delivery of limited rights data, or the Contracting Officer may require by written request the delivery of limited rights data that has been withheld or would otherwise be entitled to be withheld. If delivery of that data is required, the Contractor shall affix the following "Limited Rights Notice" to the data and the Government will treat the data, subject to the provisions of paragraphs (e) and (f) of this clause, in accordance with the notice:

LIMITED RIGHTS NOTICE (DEC 2007)

(a) These data are submitted with limited rights under Government Contract No. _____ (and subcontract ______, if appropriate). These data may be reproduced and used by the Government with the express limitation that they will not, without written permission of the Contractor, be used for purposes of manufacture nor disclosed outside the Government; except that the Government may disclose these data outside the Government for the following purposes, if any; provided that the Government makes such disclosure subject to prohibition against further use and disclosure: [Agencies may list additional purposes as set forth in 27.402-4 (c)(1) or if none, so state.]

(b) This notice shall be marked on any reproduction of these data, in whole or in part.

(End of notice)

Alternate III (Dec 2007). As prescribed in 27.409(b)(4), insert the following paragraph (g)(4) in the basic clause:

(g)(4)(i) Notwithstanding paragraph (g)(1) of this clause, the contract may identify and specify the delivery of restricted computer software, or the Contracting Officer may require by written request the delivery of restricted computer software that has been withheld or would otherwise be entitled to be withheld. If delivery of that computer software is required, the Contractor shall affix the following "Restricted Rights Notice" to the computer software and the Government will treat the computer software, subject to paragraphs (e) and (f) of this clause, in accordance with the notice:

Restricted Rights Notice (Dec 2007)

(a) This computer software is submitted with restricted rights under Government Contract No. _______ (and subcontract ________, if appropriate). It may not be used, reproduced, or disclosed by the Government except as provided in paragraph (b) of this notice or as otherwise expressly stated in the contract.

(b) This computer software may be –

(1) Used or copied for use with the computer(s) for which it was acquired, including use at any Government installation to which the computer(s) may be transferred;

(2) Used or copied for use with a backup computer if any computer for which it was acquired is inoperative;

(3) Reproduced for safekeeping (archives) or backup purposes;

(4) Modified, adapted, or combined with other computer software, provided that the modified, adapted, or combined portions of the derivative software incorporating any of the delivered, restricted computer software shall be subject to the same restricted rights;

(5) Disclosed to and reproduced for use by support service Contractors or their subcontractors in accordance with paragraphs (b)(1) through (4) of this notice; and

(6) Used or copied for use with a replacement computer.

(c) Notwithstanding the foregoing, if this computer software is copyrighted computer software, it is licensed to the Government with the minimum rights set forth in paragraph (b) of this notice.

(d) Any other rights or limitations regarding the use, duplication, or disclosure of this computer software are to be expressly stated in, or incorporated in, the contract.

(e) This notice shall be marked on any reproduction of this computer software, in whole or in part.

(End of notice)

(ii) Where it is impractical to include the Restricted Rights Notice on restricted computer software, the following short-form notice may be used instead:

Restricted Rights Notice Short Form (Jun 1987)

Use, reproduction, or disclosure is subject to restrictions set forth in Contract No. _______ (and subcontract, if appropriate) with ________ (name of Contractor and subcontractor).

(End of notice)

(iii) If restricted computer software is delivered with the copyright notice of 17 U.S.C. 401, it will be presumed to be licensed to the Government without disclosure prohibitions, with the minimum rights set forth in paragraph (b) of this clause.

Alternate IV (Dec 2007). As prescribed in 27.409(b)(5), substitute the following paragraph (c)(1) for paragraph (c)(1) of the basic clause:

(c) Copyright

> (1) Data first produced in the performance of the contract. Except as otherwise specifically provided in this contract, the Contractor may assert copyright in any data first produced in the performance of this contract. When asserting copyright, the Contractor shall affix the applicable copyright notice of 17 U.S.C. 401 or 402, and an acknowledgment of Government sponsorship (including contract number), to the data when such data are delivered to the Government, as well as when the data are published or deposited for registration as a published work in the U.S. Copyright Office. For data other than computer software, the Contractor grants to the Government, and others acting on its behalf, a paid-up, nonexclusive, irrevocable, worldwide license for all such data to reproduce, prepare derivative works, distribute copies to the public, and perform publicly and display publicly, by or on behalf of the Government. For computer software, the Contractor grants to the Government and others acting on its behalf, a paid-up, nonexclusive, irrevocable, worldwide license for all such computer software to reproduce, prepare derivative works, and perform publicly and display publicly (but not to distribute copies to the public), by or on behalf of the Government.

Alternate V (Dec 2007). As prescribed in 27.409(b)(6), add the following paragraph (j) to the basic clause:

(j) The Contractor agrees, except as may be otherwise specified in this contract for specific data deliverables listed as not subject to this paragraph, that the Contracting Officer may, up to three years after acceptance of all deliverables under this contract, inspect at the Contractor's facility any data withheld pursuant to paragraph (g)(1) of this clause, for purposes of verifying the Contractor's assertion of limited rights or restricted rights status of the data or for evaluating work performance. When the Contractor whose data are to be inspected demonstrates to the Contracting Officer that there would be a possible conflict of interest if a particular representative made the inspection, the Contracting Officer shall designate an alternate inspector.

52.227-15 Representation of Limited Rights Data and Restricted Computer Software

As prescribed in 27.409(c), insert the following provision:

REPRESENTATION OF LIMITED RIGHTS DATA AND RESTRICTED COMPUTER SOFTWARE (DEC 2007)

(a) This solicitation sets forth the Government's known delivery requirements for data (as defined in the clause at 52.227-14, Rights in Data – General). Any resulting contract may also provide the Government the option to order additional data under the Additional Data Requirements clause at 52.227-16, if included in the contract. Any data delivered under the resulting contract will be subject to the Rights in Data – General clause at 52.227-14 included in this contract. Under the latter clause, a Contractor may withhold from delivery data that qualify as limited rights data or restricted computer software, and deliver form, fit, and function data instead. The latter clause also may be used with its Alternates II and/or III to obtain delivery of limited rights data or restricted computer software, marked with limited rights or restricted rights notices, as appropriate. In addition, use of Alternate V with this latter clause provides the Government the right to inspect such data at the Contractor's facility.

(b) By completing the remainder of this paragraph, the offeror represents that it has reviewed the requirements for the delivery of technical data or computer software and states [offeror check appropriate block] –

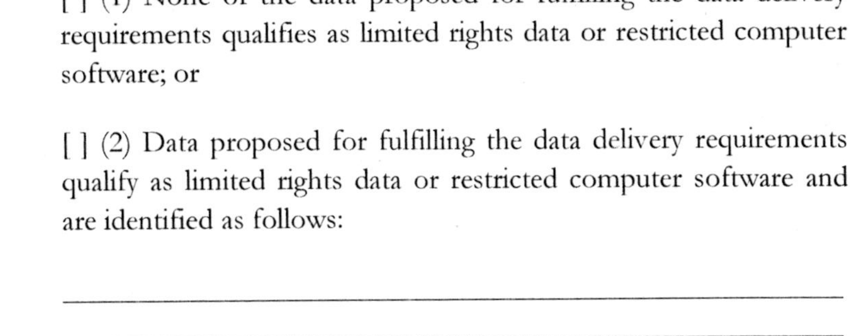

[ ] (1) None of the data proposed for fulfilling the data delivery requirements qualifies as limited rights data or restricted computer software; or

[ ] (2) Data proposed for fulfilling the data delivery requirements qualify as limited rights data or restricted computer software and are identified as follows:

____

____

(c) Any identification of limited rights data or restricted computer software in the offeror's response is not determinative of the status of the data should a contract be awarded to the offeror.

(End of provision)

52.227-16 Additional Data Requirements

As prescribed in 27.409(d), insert the following clause:

ADDITIONAL DATA REQUIREMENTS (JUNE 1987)

(a) In addition to the data (as defined in the clause at 52.227-14, Rights in Data – General clause or other equivalent included in this contract) specified elsewhere in this contract to be delivered, the Contracting Officer may, at any time during contract performance or within a period of 3 years after acceptance of all items to be delivered under this contract, order any data first produced or specifically used in the performance of this contract.

(b) The Rights in Data – General clause or other equivalent included in this contract is applicable to all data ordered under this Additional Data Requirements clause. Nothing contained in this clause shall require the Contractor to deliver any data the withholding of which is authorized by the Rights in Data – General or other equivalent clause of this contract, or data which are specifically identified in this contract as not subject to this clause.

(c) When data are to be delivered under this clause, the Contractor will be compensated for converting the data into the prescribed form, for reproduction, and for delivery.

(d) The Contracting Officer may release the Contractor from the requirements of this clause for specifically identified data items at any time during the 3-year period set forth in paragraph (a) of this clause.

52.227-17 Rights in Data – Special Works

As prescribed in 27.409(e), insert the following clause:

RIGHTS IN DATA – SPECIAL WORKS (DEC 2007)

(a) Definitions. As used in this clause –

"Data" means recorded information, regardless of form or the media on which it may be recorded. The term includes technical data and computer software. The term does not include information incidental to contract administration, such as financial, administrative, cost or pricing, or management information.

"Unlimited rights" means the rights of the Government to use, disclose, reproduce, prepare derivative works, distribute copies to the public, and perform publicly and display publicly, in any manner and for any purpose, and to have or permit others to do so.

(b) Allocation of Rights.

(1) The Government shall have –

(i) Unlimited rights in all data delivered under this contract, and in all data first produced in the performance of this contract, except as provided in paragraph (c) of this clause.

(ii) The right to limit assertion of copyright in data first produced in the performance of this contract, and to obtain assignment of copyright in that data, in accordance with paragraph (c)(1) of this clause.

(iii) The right to limit the release and use of certain data in accordance with paragraph (d) of this clause.

(2) The Contractor shall have, to the extent permission is granted in accordance with paragraph (c)(1) of this clause, the right to assert claim to copyright subsisting in data first produced in the performance of this contract.

(c) Copyright –

(1) Data first produced in the performance of this contract.

(i) The Contractor shall not assert or authorize others to assert any claim to copyright subsisting in any data first produced in the performance of this contract without prior written permission of the Contracting Officer. When copyright is asserted, the Contractor shall affix the appropriate copyright notice of 17 U.S.C. 401 or 402 and acknowledgment of Government sponsorship (including contract number) to the data when delivered to the Government, as well as when the data are published or deposited for registration as a published work in the U.S. Copyright Office. The Contractor grants to the Government, and others acting on its behalf, a paid-up, nonexclusive, irrevocable, worldwide license for all delivered data to reproduce, prepare derivative works, distribute copies to the public, and perform publicly and display publicly, by or on behalf of the Government.

(ii) If the Government desires to obtain copyright in data first produced in the performance of this contract and permission has not been granted as set forth in paragraph (c)(1)(i) of this clause, the Contracting Officer shall direct the Contractor to assign (with or without registration), or obtain the assignment of, the copyright to the Government or its designated assignee.

(2) Data not first produced in the performance of this contract. The Contractor shall not, without prior written permission of the Contracting Officer, incorporate in data delivered under this contract any data not first produced in the performance of this contract and that contain the copyright notice of 17 U.S.C. 401 or

402, unless the Contractor identifies such data and grants to the Government, or acquires on its behalf, a license of the same scope as set forth in paragraph (c)(1) of this clause.

(d) Release and use restrictions. Except as otherwise specifically provided for in this contract, the Contractor shall not use, release, reproduce, distribute, or publish any data first produced in the performance of this contract, nor authorize others to do so, without written permission of the Contracting Officer.

(e) Indemnity. The Contractor shall indemnify the Government and its officers, agents, and employees acting for the Government against any liability, including costs and expenses, incurred as the result of the violation of trade secrets, copyrights, or right of privacy or publicity, arising out of the creation, delivery, publication, or use of any data furnished under this contract; or any libelous or other unlawful matter contained in such data. The provisions of this paragraph do not apply unless the Government provides notice to the Contractor as soon as practicable of any claim or suit, affords the Contractor an opportunity under applicable laws, rules, or regulations to participate in the defense of the claim or suit, and obtains the Contractor's consent to the settlement of any claim or suit other than as required by final decree of a court of competent jurisdiction; and these provisions do not apply to material furnished to the Contractor by the Government and incorporated in data to which this clause applies.

(End of clause)

52.227-18 Rights in Data – Existing Works

As prescribed in 27.409(f), insert the following clause:

RIGHTS IN DATA – EXISTING WORKS (DEC 2007)

(a) Except as otherwise provided in this contract, the Contractor grants to the Government, and others acting on its behalf, a paid-up nonexclusive, irrevocable, worldwide license to reproduce, prepare derivative works, and perform publicly and display publicly, by or on behalf of the Government, for all the material or subject matter called for under this contract, or for which this clause is specifically made applicable.

(b) The Contractor shall indemnify the Government and its officers, agents, and employees acting for the Government against any liability, including costs and expenses, incurred as the result of (1) the violation of trade secrets, copyrights, or right of privacy or publicity, arising out of the creation, delivery, publication or use of any data furnished under this contract; or (2) any libelous or other unlawful matter contained in such data. The provisions of this paragraph do not apply unless the Government provides notice to the Contractor as soon as practicable of any claim or suit, affords the Contractor an opportunity under applicable laws, rules, or regulations to participate in the defense of the claim or suit, and obtains the Contractor's consent to the settlement of any claim or suit other than as required by final decree of a court of competent jurisdiction; and do not apply to material furnished to the Contractor by the Government and incorporated in data to which this clause applies.

(End of clause)

52.227-19 Commercial Computer Software License

As prescribed in 27.409(g), insert the following clause:

COMMERCIAL COMPUTER SOFTWARE LICENSE (DEC 2007)

(a) Notwithstanding any contrary provisions contained in the Contractor's standard commercial license or lease agreement, the Contractor agrees that the Government will have the rights that are set forth in paragraph (b) of this clause to use, duplicate or disclose any commercial computer software delivered under this contract. The terms and provisions of this contract shall comply with Federal laws and the Federal Acquisition Regulation.

(b)

(1) The commercial computer software delivered under this contract may not be used, reproduced, or disclosed by the Government except as provided in paragraph (b)(2) of this clause or as expressly stated otherwise in this contract.

(2) The commercial computer software may be –

(i) Used or copied for use with the computer(s) for which it was acquired, including use at any Government installation to which the computer(s) may be transferred;

(ii) Used or copied for use with a backup computer if any computer for which it was acquired is inoperative;

(iii) Reproduced for safekeeping (archives) or backup purposes;

(iv) Modified, adapted, or combined with other computer software, provided that the modified, adapted, or combined portions of the derivative software incorporating any of the delivered, commercial computer software shall be subject to same restrictions set forth in this contract;

(v) Disclosed to and reproduced for use by support service Contractors or their subcontractors, subject to the same restrictions set forth in this contract; and

(vi) Used or copied for use with a replacement computer.

(3) If the commercial computer software is otherwise available without disclosure restrictions, the Contractor licenses it to the Government without disclosure restrictions.

(c) The Contractor shall affix a notice substantially as follows to any commercial computer software delivered under this contract:

Notice-Notwithstanding any other lease or license agreement that may pertain to, or accompany the delivery of, this computer software, the rights of the Government regarding its use, reproduction and disclosure are as set forth in Government Contract No.______________________________.

(End of clause)

52.227-20 Rights in Data – SBIR Program

As prescribed in 27.409(h), insert the following clause:

RIGHTS IN DATA – SBIR PROGRAM (DEC 2007)

(a) Definitions. As used in this clause –

"Computer database" or "database" means a collection of recorded information in a form capable of, and for the purpose of, being stored in, processed, and operated on by a computer. The term does not include computer software.

"Computer software" –

> (1) Means.
>
> > (i) Computer programs that comprise a series of instructions, rules, routines, or statements, regardless of the media in which recorded, that allow or cause a computer to perform a specific operation or series of operations; and
> >
> > (ii) Recorded information comprising source code listings, design details, algorithms, processes, flow charts, formulas, and related material that would enable the computer program to be produced, created, or compiled.
>
> (2) Does not include computer databases or computer software documentation.

"Computer software documentation" means owner's manuals, user's manuals, installation instructions, operating instructions, and other similar items, regardless of storage medium, that explain the capabilities of the computer software or provide instructions for using the software.

"Data" means recorded information, regardless of form or the media on which it may be recorded. The term includes technical data and computer software. The term does not include information incidental to contract administration, such as financial, administrative, cost or pricing or management information.

"Form, fit, and function data" means data relating to items, components, or processes that are sufficient to enable physical and functional interchangeability, and data identifying source, size, configuration, mating and attachment characteristics, functional characteristics, and performance requirements. For computer software it means data identifying source, functional characteristics, and performance requirements but specifically excludes the source code, algorithms, processes, formulas, and flow charts of the software.

"Limited rights data" means data (other than computer software) developed at private expense that embody trade secrets or are commercial or financial and confidential or privileged.

"Restricted computer software" means computer software developed at private expense and that is a trade secret, is commercial or financial and confidential or privileged, or is copyrighted computer software, including minor modifications of the computer software.

"SBIR data" means data first produced by a Contractor that is a small business concern in performance of a small business innovation research contract issued under the authority of 15 U.S.C. 638, which data are not generally known, and which data without obligation as to its confidentiality have not been made available to others by the Contractor or are not already available to the Government.

"SBIR rights" means the rights in SBIR data set forth in the SBIR Rights Notice of paragraph (d) of this clause.

"Technical data" means recorded information (regardless of the form or method of the recording) of a scientific or technical nature (including computer databases and computer software documentation). This term does not include computer software or financial, administrative, cost or pricing, or management data or other information incidental to contract administration. The term includes recorded information of a scientific or technical nature that is included in computer databases. (See 41 U.S.C. 403(8).)

"Unlimited rights" means the right of the Government to use, disclose, reproduce, prepare derivative works, distribute copies to the public, and perform publicly and display publicly, in any manner and for any purpose whatsoever, and to have or permit others to do so.

(b) Allocation of rights.

(1) Except as provided in paragraph (c) of this clause regarding copyright, the Government shall have unlimited rights in –

(i) Data specifically identified in this contract as data to be delivered without restriction;

(ii) Form, fit, and function data delivered under this contract;

(iii) Data delivered under this contract (except for restricted computer software) that constitute manuals or instructional and training material for installation, operation, or routine maintenance and repair of items, components, or processes delivered or furnished for use under this contract; and

(iv) All other data delivered under this contract unless provided otherwise for SBIR data in accordance with paragraph (d) of this clause or for limited rights data or restricted computer software in accordance with paragraph (f) of this clause.

(2) The Contractor shall have the right to –

(i) Assert copyright in data first produced in the performance of this contract to the extent provided in paragraph (c)(1) of this clause;

(ii) Protect SBIR rights in SBIR data delivered under this contract in the manner and to the extent provided in paragraph (d) of this clause;

(iii) Substantiate use of, add, or correct SBIR rights or copyright notices and to take other appropriate action, in accordance with paragraph (e) of this clause; and

(iv) Withhold from delivery those data which are limited rights data or restricted computer software to the extent provided in paragraph (f) of this clause.

(c) Copyright –

(1) Data first produced in the performance of this contract.

(i) Except as otherwise specifically provided in this contract, the Contractor may assert copyright subsisting in any data first produced in the performance of this contract.

(ii) When asserting copyright, the Contractor shall affix the applicable copyright notice of 17 U.S.C. 401 or 402 and an acknowledgment of Government sponsorship (including contract number).

(iii) For data other than computer software, the Contractor grants to the Government, and others acting on its behalf, a paid-up nonexclusive, irrevocable, worldwide license to reproduce, prepare derivative works, distribute copies to the public, and perform publicly and display publicly, by or on behalf of the Government. For computer software, the Contractor grants to the Government, and others acting on its behalf, a paid-up, nonexclusive, irrevocable, worldwide license in such copyrighted computer software to reproduce, prepare derivative works, and perform publicly and display publicly, by or on behalf of the Government.

(2) Data not first produced in the performance of this contract. The Contractor shall not, without prior written permission of the Contracting Officer, incorporate in data delivered under this contract any data that are not first produced in the performance of

this contract unless the Contractor (i) identifies such data and (ii) grants to the Government, or acquires on its behalf, a license of the same scope as set forth in paragraph (c)(1) of this clause.

(3) Removal of copyright notices. The Government will not remove any copyright notices placed on data pursuant to this paragraph (c), and will include such notices on all reproductions of the data.

(d) Rights to SBIR data.

(1) The Contractor is authorized to affix the following "SBIR Rights Notice" to SBIR data delivered under this contract and the Government will treat the data, subject to the provisions of paragraphs (e) and (f) of this clause, in accordance with the notice:

SBIR RIGHTS NOTICE (DEC 2007)

These SBIR data are furnished with SBIR rights under Contract No._____ (and subcontract _____, if appropriate). For a period of 4 years, unless extended in accordance with FAR 27.409(h), after acceptance of all items to be delivered under this contract, the Government will use these data for Government purposes only, and they shall not be disclosed outside the Government (including disclosure for procurement purposes) during such period without permission of the Contractor, except that, subject to the foregoing use and disclosure prohibitions, these data may be disclosed for use by support Contractors. After the protection period, the Government has a paid-up license to use, and to authorize others to use on its behalf, these data for Government purposes, but is relieved of all disclosure prohibitions and assumes no liability for unauthorized use of these data by third parties. This notice shall be affixed to any reproductions of these data, in whole or in part.

(END OF NOTICE)

(2) The Government's sole obligation with respect to any SBIR data shall be as set forth in this paragraph (d).

(e) Omitted or incorrect markings.

(1) Data delivered to the Government without any notice authorized by paragraph (d) of this clause shall be deemed to have been furnished with unlimited rights. The Government assumes no liability for the disclosure, use, or reproduction of such data.

(2) If the unmarked data has not been disclosed without restriction outside the Government, the Contractor may request, within 6 months (or a longer time approved by the Contracting Officer in writing for good cause shown) after delivery of the data, permission to have authorized notices placed on the data at the Contractor's expense, and the Contracting Officer may agree to do so if the Contractor –

(i) Identifies the data to which the omitted notice is to be applied;

(ii) Demonstrates that the omission of the notice was inadvertent;

(iii) Establishes that the use of the proposed notice is authorized; and

(iv) Acknowledges that the Government has no liability with respect to the disclosure or use of any such data made prior to the addition of the notice or resulting from the omission of the notice.

(3) If the data has been marked with an incorrect notice, the Contracting Officer may –

(i) Permit correction of the notice at the Contractor's expense, if the Contractor identifies the data and demonstrates that the correct notice is authorized; or

(ii) Correct any incorrect notices.

(f) Protection of limited rights data and restricted computer software. The Contractor may withhold from delivery qualifying limited rights data and restricted computer software that are not identified in paragraphs (b)(1)(i), (ii), and (iii) of this clause. As a condition to this withholding, the Contractor shall identify the data being withheld, and furnish form, fit, and function data instead.

(g) Subcontracting. The Contractor shall obtain from its subcontractors all data and rights therein necessary to fulfill the Contractor's obligations to the Government under this contract. If a subcontractor refuses to accept terms affording the Government those rights, the Contractor shall promptly notify the Contracting Officer of the refusal and not proceed with the subcontract award without further authorization in writing from the Contracting Officer.

(h) Relationship to patents. Nothing contained in this clause shall imply a license to the Government under any patent or be construed as affecting the scope of any license or other right otherwise granted to the Government.

(End of clause)

52.227-21 Technical Data Declaration, Revision, and Withholding of Payment – Major Systems

As prescribed in 27.409(j), insert the following clause:

TECHNICAL DATA DECLARATION, REVISION, AND WITHHOLDING OF PAYMENT – MAJOR SYSTEMS (DEC 2007)

(a) Scope of declaration. The Contractor shall provide, in accordance with 41 U.S.C. 418a (d)(7), the following declaration with respect to all technical data that relate to a major system and that are delivered or required to be delivered under this contract or that are delivered within 3 years after acceptance of all items (other than technical data) delivered under this contract unless a different period is set forth in the contract. The Contracting Officer may release the Contractor from all or part of the requirements of this clause for specifically identified technical data items at any time during the period covered by this clause.

(b) Technical data declaration.

(1) All technical data that are subject to this clause shall be accompanied by the following declaration upon delivery:

TECHNICAL DATA DECLARATION (JAN 1997)

The Contractor, ________________, hereby declares that, to the best of its knowledge and belief, the technical data delivered herewith under Government contract No. _______ (and subcontract ________________, if appropriate) are complete, accurate, and comply with the requirements of the contract concerning such technical data.

(END OF DECLARATION)

(2) The Government may, at any time during the period covered by this clause, direct correction of any deficiencies that are not in compliance with contract requirements. The corrections shall be made at the expense of the Contractor. Unauthorized markings on data shall not be considered a deficiency for the purpose of this clause, but will be treated in accordance with paragraph (e) of the Rights in Data – General clause included in this contract.

(c) Technical data revision. The Contractor also shall, at the request of the Contracting Officer, revise technical data that are subject to this clause to reflect engineering design changes made during the performance of this contract and affecting the form, fit, and function of any item (other than technical data) delivered under this contract. The Contractor may submit a request for an equitable adjustment to the terms and conditions of this contract for any revisions to technical data made pursuant to this paragraph.

(d) Withholding of payment.

(1) At any time before final payment under this contract the Contracting Officer may withhold payment as a reserve up to an amount not exceeding $100,000 or 5 percent of the amount of this contract, whichever is less, if the Contractor fails to –

(i) Make timely delivery of the technical data;

(ii) Provide the declaration required by paragraph (b)(1) of this clause;

(iii) Make the corrections required by paragraph (b)(2) of this clause; or

(iv) Make revisions requested under paragraph (c) of this clause.

(2) The Contracting Officer may withhold the reserve until the Contractor has complied with the direction or requests of the Contracting Officer or determines that the deficiencies relating to delivered data, arose out of causes beyond the control of the Contractor and without the fault or negligence of the Contractor.

(3) The withholding of any reserve under this clause, or the subsequent payment of the reserve, shall not be construed as a waiver of any Government rights.

(End of clause)

52.227-22 Major System – Minimum Rights

As prescribed in 27.409(k), insert the following clause:

MAJOR SYSTEM – MINIMUM RIGHTS (JUNE 1987)

Notwithstanding any other provision of this contract, the Government shall have unlimited rights in any technical data, other than computer software, developed in the performance of this contract and relating to a major system or supplies for a major system procured or to be procured by the Government, to the extent that delivery of such technical data is required as an element of performance under this contract. The rights of the Government under this clause are in addition to and not in lieu of its rights under the other provisions of this contract.

(End of clause)

52.227-23 Rights to Proposal Data (Technical)

As prescribed in 27.409(l), insert the following clause:

RIGHTS TO PROPOSAL DATA (TECHNICAL) (JUNE 1987)

Except for data contained on pages _____, it is agreed that as a condition of award of this contract, and notwithstanding the conditions of any notice appearing thereon, the Government shall have unlimited rights (as defined in the "Rights in Data – General" clause contained in this contract) in and to the technical data contained in the proposal dated ____________, upon which this contract is based.

(End of clause)

Courtesy of William C. Bergmann, Baker Hostetler LLP

ASPATORE